Meeka Walsh, in her travel journals, locates the disruptions of place and the marvellous integrities of her responding self. The sites of her homing and unhoming are as various as Winnipeg and New York and Rome, as complex as Israel and Russia. Her seeing is profoundly Canadian in its will at once to document and to imagine. And in her writing style, in the passionate care of her language, Meeka Walsh maps the reader into those magical landscapes where place and vision fuse.

—Robert Kroetsch

Meeka Walsh has an amazingly quick-witted ability to make vivid pictures with her words.

—Wanda Koop

I0807589

Ordinary Magic:
Intervals in a Life

Ordinary Magic: Intervals in a Life

MEEKA WALSH

TURNSTONE PRESS

Turnstone Press gratefully acknowledges the assistance of the Manitoba Arts Council and the Canada Council.

Turnstone Press
607-100 Arthur Street
Winnipeg, Manitoba
Canada R3B 1H3

Cover design: Robert MacDonald, MediaClones

Front cover photo: Robert Enright

This book was printed by Hignell Printing Limited for Turnstone Press.

Printed and bound in Canada.

Canadian Cataloguing in Publication Data

Walsh, Meeka

Ordinary magic

ISBN 0-88801-136-9

1. Walsh, Meeka—Journeys. 2. Walsh, Meeka—Diaries. 3. Voyages and travels—1981-. I. Title.

PS8595.A48Z53 1989 910.4 C89-098032-2
PR9199.3.W34Z47 1989

ACKNOWLEDGEMENTS

As with any project there are a number of people to whom I owe thanks but three people have been especially helpful in bringing this book to publication: Deborah Russell, who typed the manuscript with accuracy and good spirits; Pat Sanders, a Turnstone editor who has responded to my writing with encouragement from the beginning; and finally David Arnason, whose extraordinary editorial skills have helped make this a better book.

Selections from the Israel, Rome journals were published in *Border Crossings* in the fall of 1986. In December 1987, selections from the Russian journals were read by the author on the C.B.C radio program, "Arts Encounters."

for Robert who said “write”

CONTENTS

PREFACE

The journal form is a curious one. Written in the first person, it is at once both exclusive and generous—the exclusivity coming from the personal and singular observations, the generosity coming from the obvious willingness to share. Because no matter how narrow the intended audience or how intimate and close the confidences, journals are written to be read—by someone. While not addressing a "dear reader," the journal writer has in mind the notion that the words will be read and the perceptions received by a reader who is not only interested and tolerant but also "dear."

The intent in writing *Ordinary Magic* wasn't different. It wasn't written as a single whole piece. The writing took place over three years during which time my life changed sufficiently for it to seem to me that the book hadn't been written by the same hand. But it was. I've read it all through now, have stepped back into the little distance that type on paper has allowed, and I am interested as a reader to note the differences in the writing. When I wrote the Israeli section I hadn't thought about the journal form, hadn't considered the possibilities, didn't know what the journal could be. I was formal with it, a little wary, not sure what was allowed. I remembered my mother, always careful, always cautioning against committing things to permanent record, a record which could be discovered and held as evidence. The charges which could follow were never outlined. Just the caution never to commit anything to paper that you didn't want read.

Of course now I understand that journals are written precisely for that reason—to be read. But then, I wasn't sure and I felt bold and a little nervy. How brazen of me to commit thoughts and observations to paper. How bold to be cranky on the page. How brash to think the works were worth recording and how optimistic and hopeful too.

Now I know more about the form. I've read and read: the journals of insiders and outsiders; journals written in the nineteenth century, and some written almost yesterday; some which were examples of glassy control and others written with abandon; travel journals and minute household observations; the writing of celebrated literary figures and people just trying to determine who they are. Everything is acceptable. The rule that applies is the same rule that applies to all writing—only that the writing be good. The page belongs to the journal keeper and on it she can tell as much or as little as she chooses. The understanding is that we all live little fictions. That we allow ourselves these small graces and offer them to others too, and it's this that colours our world.

I think of hand-tinted steel engravings barely touched with colour and I think of the careful hand that applied the brush. Two people observe the same event and the difference in their perceptions is as subtle as the hand that colours those fine steel-point book plates. These small variations are the little fictions.

In my book I've written about places. I've described them and responded to them. I've talked about travel and how it feels to be in a setting that's foreign and has few recognizable reference points. In Israel, without much analysis, I simply responded. I was excited, moved, angry, proud, impatient.

As I reread the journal from this trip, which concluded with several days in Rome, I was able to identify the signs that should have indicated my marriage was faltering. In spite of my enthusiasm for what I was seeing and learning, there were intermittent expressions of grief, loneliness and anger. The writing told the signs but I wasn't reading them.

By the time I travelled to Russia my life was very different and my responses to this complicated, difficult, irresistible country were different. The Russian journal shows a more contemplative, analytical and isolated writer. I was commenting on things which were more abstract—culture, politics, the notion of time and my own nature. The writing had changed too. When I returned home I continued to write.

"Ordinary Magic" is a section written some six months later. It's a journal. Some of it could be considered memoir, some is clearly fiction.

I kept the first journal at the suggestion of someone who was my teacher and friend. He's still those things and has become, since that time, much more. That journal began on December 18, 1985. Entries continued until Paul and Zach and I left Rome for Canada on January 6, 1986. I returned to find my daughter very ill and my dear Irish Wolfhound, my dear, old friend, dying. My marriage was dying too. From that time on I did write but there was no more journal writing until I left for Russia in March of 1987. I was, however, travelling. Travelling an ordeal, not a distance. Travelling with a catch in my throat and a pain, sometimes almost beyond enduring, in my chest. It was a mean journey characterized by overwhelming disillusionment. Betrayal is nasty business. He's a black crow of a travel companion and he rides on your shoulder as you go. Lately he's lifted off and flapped away but he does come back to settle briefly, even now. He's bitter knowledge and now that I know he's there, he's there.

There are two journals here, maybe more. Read the travel, read the signs I didn't see and read the pleasure and excitement I did know. It's all travel of a sort.

The journals were written in my shiny, black, hard-covered school notebooks. In planes, on buses, in hotel rooms, restaurants, on park benches and in my study I wrote in my almost illegible hand and what appears now has been little changed.

ORDINARY MAGIC

Your life is always what's already happened. Someone says, tell me about your life, and you decide how far back you want to go but it always is back. It's rarely about now because if you stretch now too much you're into the future—the part that hasn't happened yet. So you're always talking about the past. And it's made up of days, individual days or days locked together in a sequence.

Unless you take photographs for *National Geographic* magazine most days are pretty ordinary. Most lives are pretty ordinary. You say that at cocktail parties. It's an attitude that determines your conduct at work. As a notion it's effective in combatting both arrogance and disappointment. You even say it to yourself on those occasions when personal dishonesty is called for. There are those layered, veiled situations when you lie to yourself a little. But by God you know your life isn't ordinary! Everyone else's may be, but not yours!

This is a story about an ordinary life. A day at a time. And so far it's not about the future. "Well, what about the future?" someone with no imagination will ask. "Think about it," they persist. I like to be co-operative. I was an easy child. I made no noisy trouble. Now, dog-like, I pause. I know my face becomes doggy—blank. I look forward but I can't see it.

But here's what I'll do. I'll go back and pick out some days to tell you and the telling takes time and from the beginning to the end of each small piece I'll be moving forward. There'll be a little bit of future, about as much as from the front steps to the hedge at the property line and through the white wooden gate.

When I was about nine a favourite story of mine was *The Secret Garden*. I don't recall reading it to my children for some reason so my recollections about it aren't specific, except for the secret door into the garden. My gate is special too. As soon as I'm not looking at it I believe it hangs unsupported. I know it does. There's a hedge along the front of my garden, dividing it from the street. It's interrupted by a tidy, perfect, white wooden gate and I swear that gate just hangs there, hovering in a break in the hedge right in front of my flagstone walk.

Open it. I'll make magic. I'll take all the stuff I've saved, the small observations I've made, the big anger, the grey and abrasive grief and the blue colour of a jay's tail and I'll turn it all into words.

Winnipeg, late September 1987

I began a journal entry this way. Write it out, write it away. Right it out, right it away.

I went on. I look forward to a time when writing won't be scrubbing on a washing stone, when there'll be nothing to rub away. I'm divorced today. My lawyer called and told me. Just a few papers to draft and it will be final. A few papers away to the end—of so much promise, so many promises. And no one has told me what happened or how. Not a single word exchanged with Paul, nor will there be. Silence.

Up early in the morning. The alarm intruding in the jumble which fills most nights. Exhausted, waking and feeling drugged. Lying in bed, searching for the day. Light or still dark? Raining or leaves rustling? Fall coming to a close and soon no more open windows at night, no more morning birds.

Why did I set the alarm early today? Yes—tonight is my magazine's annual board meeting. Up early to bake a chocolate cake and to finalize the agenda and my report.

Breakfast. Bake the cake, dress, walk the dog. Just as we hurry up the steps the phone rings.

It's my lawyer. "You're divorced. He filed in July. Soon it will be final." I'm pleasant, light. It's expected. Be social, be appropriate, easy.

My cake needs a glaze. Rum in a pot, cocoa powder, icing sugar. My kitchen-past is baking this cake. Drizzle and cover. Leave a note cautioning Zach against eating it. Promise him his own. I'd bake him the world.

To the bank where some error with mortgage payments has been made. Now, any irregularities appear like threats. It's as though people are jumping out at me from around a corner with a scream or a bad face.

The bank person who is probably my daughter's age calls me by my first name. I don't know what's in her bank account. I don't know her first name. We adjust the small error and I'm on track again.

To the office. Phone calls, letters, papers for the meeting. To the typesetter to look at final pages for the next magazine. Pleasant, light, smiling. Home, exhausted almost into immobility in the car. Walk the dog.

My stomach is raw. A fist of bread and a cup of milk to fill the hole. I take it into the dining-room and sit on one of the straight-backed chairs. I need the deep blue of that room. The eternal blue of the walls.

Shower and change clothes and back to the office for the meeting. Nice people, good people. I'm glad to see them all.

Coming home alone later I realize again that today I'm divorced. I take the dog out and walk. The yellow leaves pushed up against the street lights transfer the light and it becomes yellow. The drier brown leaves sound like water. One street over, an old man lives alone and keeps an impeccable garden. Flowers and vegetables.

Prudently, he's emptied the vegetable garden, turned it over for next spring. I'm relieved that habit has extended his life. It could take him through the winter. Future time.

All he's left of his corn rows are six tall stalks. The leaves are dry and long as the hands of a pre-Raphaelite girl. Their sound is picked out from all the others. Who's reading papers in the garden at night? Who's out there rustling? The dog and I both stop and look into the garden. We listen to the paper leaves, dry anxious hands. Then we walk on.

I'll go to bed now. I'll take an apple and read and then I'll sleep.

One day, almost mid-October

It's 9:00 in the evening. I'm at my writing table in the room I've made perfect for myself. I was allowed to keep the oak kitchen table. I had had it designed and made just the way I wanted it. It's a small refactory table, the colour of beeswax. The top is the thickness of a good book. It weighs more than one man can lift and now fits perfectly in front of the double windows in the room designated as my study. I've laid one of Gramma's Persian rugs on the floor. Three walls have book shelves floor to ceiling and a black Windsor rocker that lived here before I bought the house sits in a corner in front of the books. The last time I toured this house before deciding to buy it, Robert had seen me eyeing the chair. He made secret arrangements, tied a blue ribbon on it and three days later surprised me with it on my birthday.

October evening in my study, I'm at my writing table in front of the open windows. The part of the world I love best is just that amount that filters through my open windows. It's 9:00 p.m., quiet and dark, unusually warm for October and someone is out in the night raking leaves. I can hear the lovely brushing sound. The night becomes a mole's tunnel and we live inside it as happily as we do in our diurnal habitat.

This morning at the riding club just outside the bunkhouse, my foot brushed something soft. I looked down and there at my toe lay a small, finely coloured bird, smaller than a sparrow. Grey and black wings, yellow belly, black and white markings at its head. Its naked pink feet were stretched, flexed away from its body, and its breathing was quick. With a thin piece of wooden shingle I lifted it up and laid it in the long grass at the side of the door. I went into the bunkhouse and when I came out minutes later the bird lay dead. The loss of that small bird in the fall of the year has scooped a hollow inside me that's there even now.

After I rode my horse I drove to the garden nursery just a mile past the stable to buy bulbs for the garden and some to ease the white winter indoors. A peach hyacinth rests in my vegetable crisper where it has to be cold-forced for twelve weeks. Then I'll bring it out, set it in a bulb vase, water it and wait. Three paper-white narcissuses can be planted on stones now. In six weeks they'll give me back some green and scent. The rest I'll hurry to plant before the snow and I'll be smug through the winter, knowing I've tended the future a little.

I bought birdseed there too. Guaranteed to lure cardinals and blue jays. In Winnipeg it would as likely produce a cardinal if I planted and watered the seed. I also bought a metal post to which I'll attach the cedar bird-feeder my kids gave me, and pounds of regular seed for the regular guys who just hang around all winter without any flash or fancy.

For dinner I roasted a monster chicken with stuffing and stuff, one day late for Thanksgiving. Zach phoned to say he'd be eating pizza with friends instead. I moved the dishes from the dining-room to the kitchen and reset the table/island there. At 6:30 Zach shuffled in saying his plans had changed and for the second time I set the table in the dining-room, delighted. I love that kid. I find him charming, witty, entertaining. I'm his mother. Objectively, his manners are bad, he's often rude and usually indifferent. It doesn't matter. I love him and know with certainty he's going to end up special.

Now I'll walk the dog into the still night. My neighbour's leaves have all been gathered.

Late October

That same man, the gardener, the man who knew about the future, had a woman growing in his garden. He's not like that now. He's too old and she's not there but for years and years she was. The grandest growing thing in this flat and practical prairie city. A rosy, topiary lady with a long skirt, a broad-brimmed hat, a wasp-waist and a sun umbrella.

The house is modest—small, white clapboard and, as it should be, trimmed in green. The flower gardens are broad, English style, packed with a disorderly mix of perennials and the faithless, flashy annuals for fill. Set a little to the back of one bed, set a modest distance from the street, was that woman, Green Sleeves, green everything. I was a teenager on a bike when I first saw her. Cornerwise from the gardener's house was an old fire station where we went each spring to buy our bicycle licences. So biking by one spring evening I came upon her. I didn't mention her to anyone. She was so remarkable it didn't bear speaking.

That man, the gardener, would sit at her hem and clip slowly. He'd clip at her cuff, he'd trim her hat, he'd narrow her waist. He'd mist her for aphids. He'd water her for lushness. She'd fill to his ministrations. She'd rustle at him, show him her leafy undersides—paler, ribby parts.

When I began to drive a car I'd direct my route down that street, going out of my way to do it. I'd have passengers. I'd drive them past. I'd say not a word. No one pointed her out. Was she unspeakable? Was she invisible? I never doubted her presence.

I hadn't seen her for a few years and then I bought a house one street over, and walking the dog I remembered her. She wasn't there. The old man still gardens and the gardens are fine but he must have taken her inside. Given in to the thin wrists and thin ankles, unable at the end to resist a lady.

What's there, where she used to be, is an unremarkable rose bush of medium height. The dog and I look into the garden every day but the bush persists. The lady remains discreet.

The late September journal entry began with the anticipation of a time when writing wouldn't be a writing out, rubbing on a washing stone. I think now that's probably wrong. More to "Do not go gentle into that good night" than a seeking after easeful death. A railing and grinding, often chewing the same thing over. It's there. It's part of me. I'll say it other ways, maybe transform it, but a lot of writing must be rubbing on a washing stone.

Annie Dillard's bent-winged Polyphemus moth turned up in *Pilgrim at Tinker Creek.* As a child at school she witnessed his disfigurement. She watched him emerge from his cocoon to find himself still trapped inside a glass mason jar. He couldn't stretch his damp wings full out and they dried only partly opened. His furred-bodied spirit stayed with her. She saw him crawl away, unwinged, down the drive and into her life for all time. That first writing was in 1974. She wrote about him again in *An American Childhood.* Now it was 1987. She warned that she'd told the moth before and might tell it still again.

Some things impress that way. Like a thumb pushed hard against your chest. I have those kinds of stories too.

The old gardener is deaf. Once I tried to praise his garden. To congratulate and encourage him. He couldn't hear me and it upset him. Since that time I nod and smile when I pass. I can't ask him about the topiary lady, why he neglected her, let her go, why she had to leave—spare me saying leaf. It's all right that way. I never found myself able to speak about her anyway.

New York City, November

Since last spring when I thought my life would drown me, that grief would cover me over and the last of my struggle would be expressed in a slow heavy bubble rising to the surface to open and spread away to nothing, Robert had been offering the sustaining idea of New York. New York, the city I love most, New York and the Plaza Hotel, 5:00-cocktail-light, the city that gives the intellectual nod to all of America's best ideas; the city whose pace comes closest to the tempo of my hyped heartbeat.

It's a place where anything is possible and while it's probably carelessly cruel, at the same time there's an almost touching naïveté centred at the core of its inhabitants. How else except to say that it's a naïve belief in what's possible can you explain why drivers, taxi-drivers most especially, will be lined up in a miles-long, choked roadway, honking at the car in front? Where does he think the person ahead of him can go? It has to be a belief in the notion of what's possible that accounts for that. And maybe it's this puppy-endless enthusiasm for what's next, this crocodile rapaciousness for the next deal, this absolute forthright crassness that doesn't mask anything that draws me to this city.

When a crêpey-skinned, done up, foot-tired waitress asks, "What can I get for you, honey?" for the five seconds of the asking you believe you are honey to her and she truly wants to bring you your heart's desire. It's possible.

So, throughout the packing up and dismantling of the marital property (it ceased to be a home the first time I saw my lawyer), the unsettling and settling into my new house, the preparations for the trial, the unspeakably brutalizing trial, and more, Robert would salve me, would soothe and coax me on with the thought of New York in the fall. "Think of it, babes," he'd say, "a week of art, of theatre, bookstores, good food and each other with no telephones, no lawyers." And I would. And it did help. It reminded me that New York wouldn't sink and give up just a bubble and that the energy and joy that made my heart beat would be there when the courts and Paul would leave me be.

The summer was a nightmare—ghetto-hot. I endured it. The fall was hectic. I had trial dates set right through September. The High Holidays were in October. I had to prepare for them. George Cleve was conducting the Winnipeg Symphony Orchestra and would be my house guest for a week. Susan Sontag was coming to Winnipeg to give a lecture early in November and Robert was interviewing her. So we set a date, November 14, and worked day and night to complete everything that was required of us.

Then, weary to the point of speechlessness, we boarded a plane at 6:15 on Saturday morning and by 2:00 were on the streets of New York heading for the galleries in Soho.

My father's generation were whistlers. They don't do it now, but when I was little my father whistled. He could whistle a tune, or do a kind of controlled trill, and he could whistle through his teeth. I never heard a girl or woman whistle through her teeth so I assumed there were men's teeth and women's teeth. I thought whistling was a fine accomplishment. I was happier being able to whistle than knowing how to play the piano. I felt special because, while I could only produce a straight, genderless whistle, I didn't know many kids who could do even that. I still think it's special. For one thing, it entitles you to have a dog. How can you own a dog if you can't whistle for it?

There is something else about every time I do it. It doesn't matter when, but each time I whistle I'm about ten years old, standing on McAdam Avenue where I lived, and it's around 7:30 early in May and I'm wearing bare legs.

Is it really true that not many people today know how to whistle? I'm a loud, clear whistler—the sound is clean and full. And people look at me when I call for my dogs so maybe it's true that no one does it today.

But my Dad's crowd, his contemporaries in Winnipeg and Edmonton and New York and in the movies, all knew how and did it. I thought that group had a lot of style. Post-war optimism, world-on-a-string, young-enough-to-do-it, style. They wore hats. My father looked like Bing Crosby in his. They wore loose trousers with big pockets. They always had change in their pockets. My father would settle his hand in his pocket a lot and jingle it. Natty. I thought we were rich because he had enough change to buy more 3-for-1-cent candy than I could eat in a week of recesses.

And camel-hair coats. My father wore one. Once he had a tweed peaked cap he sometimes wore to work in the winter. I called the hat Peter because I thought that was an English street-kid's name and that's what the hat looked like. My father dressed well, conservatively is how I'd describe it today. Then, I thought he dressed English which is funny because his parents were Russian.

In the summer, my mother, who had a lot of style in her own right, wore brown and white spectator pumps and always a hat to the races. One hat broke my heart, like the dead bird outside the bunkhouse door at the riding club. Something about it had a quality of having been recently alive, like some sort of bird. It had a flat crown and a shallow upturned brim. It was made of a pale, pale celadon green felt, fur felt with a lovely nap which was probably why I was sure it had been alive. All around the brim were silk leaves and small red cherries, small as wild pin cherries. I probably loved my mother more for owning that sweet hat than for anything else she's done.

They were smart as New York, my parents, and a couple of times when I was less than eleven or twelve they travelled by train to New York and Chicago too. I thought they *were* New York and Chicago. New York, especially. Even now each time I pass near the Plaza Hotel in the 5:00 light I think of my parents and how well they fit that city when I was little.

New York City, November

More than a week in New York and not a minute to write. Not the time or the inclination. The senses are only so elastic and they were stretched taut. We're at the airport now, and in the departure lounge there's a little time and the city is beginning to recede a bit, giving me just enough space to write in the slack.

Saturday was our last day. Until then the weather had been Central Park, fall leaves, walk-down-Fifth-Avenue-looking-like-the-Plaza weather. But early in the morning snow particles blew up to our window and for the first time we left the hotel in our coats.

The New York that we see as visitors, even familiar visitors, is a city of excesses. It's that way in part because of the pace we set for ourselves, the things we choose to do, what we look at, where we walk. But New York is the centre, an immense circuitry, demanding and urgent and when you're there you walk fast, you breathe shallowly, you keep moving, absorbing, feeding and contributing to the machinery.

So the weather isn't a surprise either. You want weather, here's weather. Be chic and elegant and casual and use this chestnut smoky day. You want weather. Step out and have the wind push your scarf against your mouth and cold tears into your eyes. We'd planned a long last day of walking and gallery visits. Change your plans.

We took a taxi to a special chocolate shop in the Village. My mother wanted truffles and Lilac makes the best. Then a bitter walk into Soho. There never seem to be taxis in the Village.

Of all the things we'd seen and done, of all the extraordinarily good art we'd looked at and responded to, the meals we'd eaten, the people we'd watched and talked with, the plays, the stores, and in a week of not writing, it's a funny little encounter, a small event, that pushes itself forward first.

A story then. It was almost the end of the day. We'd had a late lunch: a fish bisque of some sort, duck salad with pears, wine, and then coffee. We were warm and full and a little slowed by food. After lunch we'd looked in a gallery specializing in paintings by Russian emigrés. The proprietor had responded to our interest and pointed out a large canvas, more than ten feet long. Nude figures stretched across it. The artist, he told us, brought it out of Russia. To do that he'd had to paint a muddy landscape over the provocative surface. When he reached Paris he removed the disguising colour wash and there it was. The idea of covering and uncovering corresponded with what I knew of Russia.

We moved on to Mary Boone's gallery, scary Mary Boone of the alligator pumps and acerbic tongue. We looked at the upside-down canvasses of George Baselitz and then crossed the street to the 49th Parallel Gallery for a look at the Guido Molinari exhibition—a tasty, beautifully designed show in reds, black and whites.

Then, walking down West Broadway, a window display caught Robert's eye and we opened the door of a pricey men's clothing store. A young man in an ill-fitting attendant's uniform was posted inside to take parcels and guard against theft. We walked through the store, looked around. When we claimed our bags on the way out the attendant, who appeared to be in his early 20s, commented on the cold. It was even colder in Queens where he lived—windier, he told us. "There's no trees there anymore. They've cut them all down. All but one on our street so it's open now—windy. I've got hamsters," he pressed. "So I asked the guys to put the trees through the machine for me. Made me pull off all the leaves and branches first." I imagined hamsters wheeling eternally on log rounds, nails frayed flat by the bark. He went on. "Got me two big garbage bags full. Hell, shavings are expensive. When they come back I'm gonna get more." I remembered the one tree still standing on his street. We started to back out of the shop. His intensity was confusing. He was offering so much.

Actually, I was interested. I don't know any adults who keep hamsters. How many, I wondered. But we moved on. Jackets for $700 and a door attendant with a herd of hamsters.

We'd seen a dead rat on the sidewalk earlier in the day—

attractive, fat and sleek. Why had he died? He looked to be in his prime; and predator pigeons, meal-emboldened; and street squirrels who knew the ropes. They looked like New Yorkers. More comfortable on the streets than the dogs on leads. All the minks though—people were wearing them. Hundreds—black, long, glossy, plump.

Hamsters. What was the collective plural? A gaggle? A herd, flock, covey, brood? Are they like pups, all colours from the same litter, or do you breed for uniformity? Had Mendel turned his attention to rodents? Were they rodents? It's such a pejorative term and clearly this man had a real concern for the comfort of his. He had provided them with the shredded shade of a street in Queens to burrow in. And they were sufficiently forward in his mind for him to share with strangers. It occurred to me that maybe they were extraordinary in some way, that they were capable of some feat which eluded most hamsters. They were gifted or maybe they weren't gifted. They could be average or even below average—plodders perhaps. But maybe the guy at the door in the poorly fitting uniform was gifted. He had trained them. Together they all had a trick.

We arranged to meet under the tree on the street in Queens, on the morning of his day off at 10:00 in full sunlight. I was there a little early. I stood under the tree. It was windy. He was right. But today it wasn't cold. The light was a thin yellow. I had a clear view of the street. Then I saw him. He sat on top of a small cart. He must have designed it himself. It was no more than a raised platform on four large wooden wheels. The cart was drawn by a team of twenty-four hamsters. It wheeled slowly past me. He looked terrific. His uniform fit just so.

A book about travel, about distances covered, about departures and leave-takings. And about adventures, the scariest of which usually take place in settings that have nothing to do with tropical vegetation, wild animals or avalanches. Two of my three trips travelled were geographic, voyages through different cultures, different landscapes with foreign languages, and were measured in miles. The third trip, actually the middle one, the intervening space between foreign countries, was about travel from then to now or from then to here and was for me more radical and foreign than any destination requiring a passport.

Context counts for so much. You have your own and it's coloured by everything you've done, seen, learned, and you make the assumptions. If I'm setting out on a trip and I want you to travel with me, how much do I have to tell you to give you a context?

Maybe I'll start with an immigrant attitude in my background so thoroughly entrenched that my mother would say with pride, "My parents were born in this country," the assertion belying the security. The reality being that in Canada when my mother was growing up, was grown up and an adult during World War II, Jews were outsiders. Maybe to a childhood spent in the rich stew of Winnipeg's North End where each ethnic group was large enough to provide for itself. The numbers meant we could stick with our own, stay with what was known and sure. We would observe each other warily from the security of our own communities but for my family and friends there would be no mixing.

Maybe the fact that I'm an only child matters. There are two stock responses to growing up singular. One is a determination never to be alone and/or lonely and the other is a preference for something of an independent existence. I've never been uncomfortable with my own company.

When you're a kid you just know some things. When you get older some of them fall away. The ones that remain are significant: husbands and wives love each other; children are the most important; sacrifices build character; you must have an education; you have to belong to a synagogue; at some point when you're older and really mature you buy cemetery space; you never, never take advantage of anyone; a drink or two is okay—being drunk is not; you support the larger community but you take care of your own because no one else will; you count your blessings and remember that being idle and discontent are sins and you subscribe to the notion of *noblesse oblige* because you're fortunate and graced and therefore have a debt to pay.

Overriding all of this, the single notion which influenced me more than any other was the "do unto others" idea. If you treated people fairly, followed the rules and conducted yourself with dignity you would be dealt with in the same manner. I grew up trusting that scheme and assumed that if I followed it closely I could predict and largely control what happened to me. Behaviour and conduct would be returned in kind.

As early as my recollections begin, my mother worked. She had her own business, small to begin with, then growing and becoming more demanding. I knew I wanted to stay home when I grew up and married. And I did. I raised children and dogs. My home was a sanctuary filled with baking and wild fruit jam. I watched blue jays from my study window. I went to university. I did useful volunteer work. I worried for my friends and took care of cousins, aunts, grandparents. I lived a life, alas, no longer chic and sadder yet, no longer possible. And while Paul and I travelled with our children a fair amount, mine remained a smallish world.

Our trip to Israel in December 1985 marked the beginning of a stretch in my perception of the world. From the day we left, it stretched and stretched and was rent and the rip grew and my world fell into it, a world defined by my husband, my children, my dogs and my lovely house. A world where I was taken care of, protected, secure. A world within a larger world which I sensed I really wouldn't like all that much, a world where I believed my marriage would be for all time.

I saw that marriage as if it were a dance, a dance where the partners came together and moved in unison, where they drew apart but not so far apart that their fingertips broke contact with each other. I saw it as a dance where contact was sustained and in its endless rhythm you could come together again. I sensed a tension in the relationship. We weren't the same closed unit we had been for so many years. Things seemed to intervene. I was beginning to work and the work was challenging, engrossing, exciting. In a small way I was moving out into the world. Paul's career didn't seem to be as satisfying as it had been. He was tired, distracted. Was becoming vague and disengaged. But I felt we'd be all right. The dance would carry us.

I set out from Winnipeg with other attitudes too. I was Canadian first and while I knew this was not a country of great moral courage, especially in its failure to provide sanctuary for Jews during the Second World War, this was my country and I maintained a certain chauvinistic pride. I also understood why the establishment of the State of Israel was crucial for world Jewry and for the rest of the world recovering from a period of inhumanity no one would wish to see repeated. But I hadn't thought of Israel as my home and I hadn't shared the eagerness of so many Jews to go there. I chose my friends because they shared my interests, values and attitudes, and not because of a common background. So the trip to Israel was interesting to me mostly because my father-in-law had arranged for my son's Bar Mitzvah to take place at the Western Wall in Jerusalem and then because I loved to travel.

I was astonished at the intensity and the speed of my about-face. Once I had boarded the El Al flight in Montreal, looked around and recognized that everyone on that flight including the crew was Jewish, I was on my way home. I wondered at this response throughout the following three weeks. The feeling didn't leave, is with me still. It came as a surprise. I'm not, much to my family's concern, avidly pro-Jewish. In fact, in Winnipeg the Jewish community is not where I find myself. So the trip to Israel was a surprise—a turning-point for lots of reasons and a turn-about in my relationship to that country. My knowledge of Israel and my concerns for it have been appended to me, are a blood-fed part of me now.

The phrase with which many prayers are concluded, "Next year in Jerusalem," speaks of the spiritual and notional space Israel has occupied for Jews historically. Oxymorons aside, it became a tangible part of my consciousness and it's from here that the journal's pro-Israeli bias came.

ISRAEL 1985-1986
ROME 1986

Toronto
December 18, 1985
8:00 p.m.

Hours in a fog, in a crowd, the feeling as confusing as if I were in another country. Travelling since 7:00 a.m. when the alarm woke me, this day belonging to travel even before the travelling began. And still in Canada, in Toronto, surrounded by strangers, and by Paul, Zach, my father-in-law, my aunt and uncle, and all the others, all leaving what's familiar behind. Paul's stepmother Irene has done some vacationing on her own in her native Yugoslavia and will meet us in Jerusalem. Other family members will join us later.

Each flight has been delayed, this one on a wide-bodied plane filled with French, Germans, Israelis and Canadians. Across the aisle a man in a denim jacket reads a newspaper printed in Hebrew and he's comfortable enough about that to open it full out—he's already close to home. That's the first rush of feeling for me. I expect the initial experiences of Israel to be like that. No more fading and blending.

And every crowded flight must have a screaming baby. It's the exchange we make for speed. We measure the distance in that kind of discomfort. Otherwise how will we know space has been covered? It keeps us conscious.

Montreal
December 19
12:01 a.m.

Either numbness induced by fatigue or a surfeit of goodwill sustains my humour. El Al flight 010 due to leave Mirabel at 11:05 has electrical difficulties of some sort. We've been on the plane since 10:30—a plane full of Jews travelling to Israel, going home.

No one sits quietly—in fact, no one sits at all. This is not an orderly community. This is a congregation of Jews entirely comfortable, me among them. The kitchens aren't serving yet but food has appeared: corned beef, pickles, herring, materialized out of a common will, and we're having a party while technicians determine whether we go or stay. In any event on El Al we're already in Israel.

9:30 a.m.

Three hours on the tarmac and finally we were ready to lift off. The plane appears to be full of families—lots of grandparents, children of all ages—and other than the pilot's interjections in Hebrew and English there's a comforting, constant, conversational din. No drunken jocularity or goofy rowdiness of the sort I've seen on other long flights, just anticipation and good spirits.

Shortly after take-off the pilot had indicated we would be served a meal, then the lights would be turned off and we should sleep, that during the period of sleep there would be turbulence. We should stay in our seats if we awoke. Otherwise he would wake us when he wanted us to have breakfast and with that the steward closed all the window blinds and we were off.

Supper—fish with olives and lemon, salad, veal, bread rolls passed throughout, fruit and juice. Where's the usual shaving-cream dessert? Breakfast—oranges, bagels and cream cheese with smoked salmon and wonderful coffee. I feel entirely taken care of on this flight, the largest plane I've been on—400 people in a commonality that for me has previously existed only in a synagogue.

Jerusalem
6:00 p.m.

We landed in Tel Aviv in the dark and travelled in a taxi motorcade to Jerusalem. The windows were fogged and clouded by a long-awaited rain so I still had a sense of travel by air and no sense at all of where I was until we drew up in front of the King David Hotel. It's a massive limestone fortress. It could be Florence's Uffizi in expanded scale, not built in the 1930s but four or five centuries before that. Grand, impressive and elegant, a suitable setting for Israeli foreign high-level meetings and apparently bombed by the Israelis in the 1948 War of Independence because it was British headquarters.

We have a suite with arched windows through which we see the old walled city of Jerusalem. Within it is the Western Wall, the focus of our trip here.

The city appears to be built on a series of hills which today are grey-green. Directly below our windows is a golf-green lawn with clipped shrubbery and rose gardens, an olympic-sized swimming pool and tennis courts. Through the window of the sitting-room I look down into the street and there I see a stoutish man sweeping. On his head he wears a *keepah*.

December 20

Blue Jerusalem sky through an open arched window. Jerusalem birds offering more and me in my bed, on starched linen sheets, not sure what I should offer in return. I learned soon. A vague, wasted morning spent with the women, looking into jewellery shop windows while newly claimed East Jerusalem shimmered just beyond the immediacy of purchases to be made. The men had gone off to do their business, the preparation for entry into Jewish manhood. Window-shopping wasn't what I wanted. Zach is my son. Until he entered elementary school we'd spent almost all our time together. He didn't enjoy organized activity then, or now, and while other kids were in nursery school and Beavers and Cubs we hung out together and I loved it. Later, when he was "big" and in school full days his interests shifted to the kinds of things guys like to do with other guys and that was fine. But I was still there after four, and there during all the other stuff: pneumonia, measles in spite of the vaccine, appendix, a wretched parasite we'd picked up in Europe that held on for six months and worried his little being into something even littler, a year in a body cast, a year of physiotherapists and the usual run of viruses. This was my kid and shopping with the ladies wasn't what I wanted. And this was Israel, Jerusalem, not Miami or Milan. We didn't come here for the shopping. Frustration and impatience began to tap their feet.

The afternoon should have been better and a lot of it was. An over-large bus complete with socialist tour guide waited for us. The guide, Avi, was maybe 5'8", 5'9", bouncy, athletic and full of enthusiasm. If he was repeating his tour-guide's litany, that wasn't how he sounded. He was talking about his country, its achievements, its vulnerability. He spoke with urgency. Time is only one of the enemies Israel continually faces, he told us. Diaspora Jews on vacation needed to know that all of Israel could be a war zone. That security is never possible. And visitors should recognize the country's achievements in the face of circumstances so daunting and unremitting as to have no parallels in North American experience.

Born in Argentina, he emigrated to Israel as a teenager. In his job as a tour guide he met people wealthy enough to travel and vacation for substantial periods. Most were North American. Without being rude he peppered his touring commentary with clever digs at comfort, ease and the softening seduction of materialism. He was fun. I liked him.

This was my first look at Israel even if it was from the windows of a bus. I was excited and expected a lot. I got a lot and the afternoon was perfect but for a window bar running the length of the bus and set at eye level so that to see you had to scrunch or crane, perfect but for speed of passage too swift for my eyes to light and enter, to absorb and hold images. Instead they were dizzyingly deflected from surface to surface.

What was good? Travelling two miles, a distance of some reckoning in this finger-spit of land, to the wilderness, to the West Bank to see a hopeful community, modern, almost luxurious, which had been Jordan, which had been wasteland, desert, useless; now green and peopled.

I love these people, their audacity—how dare they! With the confidence of rectitude they turn sand into green so it's theirs. And the rest of the world, the temperate world, the reasoned, the fair, the liberal, would give it back to Jordan, to turn it back to sand, to be at one with the Crusaders and the Turks who turned it from forests into sand before.

So that was good.

And Bethlehem was good but surprising because it's tinsel and tourists and is that what it's all about? The Church of the Nativity, a holy site for Catholics, Greek Orthodox, the Armenian Church, is falling down, is crumbling and tarnished and only recently have the mosaics of Constantine been restored. It's ironic that they have been restored since the Israelis took over Bethlehem in 1967.

The Tomb of Rachel, the only Israeli-held shrine in Bethlehem, is on one side of the highway. On the other is a commercial building selling olive-wood souvenirs. On top of that building Israeli soldiers with machine guns in hand face Rachel's tomb to protect it. Ambiguity presents no problems here.

This evening, *Shabbat* dinner at the King David Hotel. At our table a cousin from Vancouver and some talk about publishing. His friend seated at the next table is also doing interesting things—a task force on broadcasting. Tomorrow I'll look forward to more good conversation. And tomorrow the Wall, the Bar Mitzvah. I've declined travel by taxi with the women and children and instead will walk on the Sabbath with the men into the Old City to the Wall. There I can take my secondary place with at least the pride of being out of breath and sore of foot.

December 21

Bar Mitzvah day. Everyone was tense. We had travelled such a long way. And there is no more significant place in the world to have a Bar Mitzvah than the Western Wall of the Temple, the holiest place for Jews. Here we were, about to present ourselves at this site, to participate in a ceremony bringing Zach from childhood into Jewish manhood in accordance with an unbroken historical tradition. I guess I expected the light would change, the weather would take some notice and that we all would come away altered by the experience. I've never been interested in small measures.

We rendezvoused with the others in the hotel lobby at 9:15, everyone shiny and neat. The other women and the children drove to the Wall. The rest of us set out on foot, first descending to the Jaffa gate and there, once inside the old walled city, we climbed and wound our way inward through narrow, arched, vaulted and cobbled roadways. It was the perfect approach. Finally, the path opened on a large plaza and there at the far end stood the Wall. First we must pass through an Israeli check-point and empty our bags. Then our *tallit* bags are searched. Now we can approach. The Wall has an almost human presence, wide, impassive, receptive, tolerant and prevailing. A section is cordoned off for women who, in this orthodox setting, are separated from the men. Zach was to have his service adjacent to the barrier so I was close. I could almost touch him and didn't feel much removed.

Surrounding us were groups of strangers conducting their own services, each at a different point in the ceremony so there was a distracting din which at the same time was not inappropriate. But of the people Paul's father and Irene invited, few even remained silent during Zach's reading. I found myself annoyed that they would continue to chat and visit in full voice. What should have been an occasion for high emotion and religious celebration instead was interrupted by this irritation.

Zach conducted himself well and seemed content with his

portion. The men were allowed entrance into the synagogue and were secreted away to an area where the women weren't admitted. I was proud of this self-possessed little being and pleased that the Bar Mitzvah ceremony hadn't disappointed him.

At one point when the men withdrew I approached the Wall with my prayer. Each crevice is stuffed with bits of folded paper covered in other prayers. The stones are smooth to the touch from desperate and pleading hands wandering over them. There is a comfort in transmitting worship to an object—dangerous stuff, that.

Paul, Zach, Paul's cousin R. and his friend and I walked around the Arab section a bit after everyone left. We circled the Mosque of the Dome of the Rock, wishing for more time to look, and then taxied back to the hotel for a celebratory lunch. It was lavish and good. A lot of the meals here are buffet and this was another. The dining-room set aside for the Walshes' party was a handsome wood-panelled room and the ceiling was patterned to look not unlike the coloured tiles on the exterior of the El Aqsa Mosque—a lovely Persian blue with gold. For lunch, we were served wonderful cold fish dishes cooked in a variety of ways with tomatoes, green olives or prunes. Cold vegetable salads prepared in the Russian manner with mayonnaise, mustard sauces or vinegar and wonderful breads and cheese—a variety of both. Pastries and fruit for dessert and a huge cake with blue and white icing for Zach. I made wry note of the fact that many of the seventy or so people there hadn't attended the service, choosing lunch as the appropriate observance for a Bar Mitzvah. Well, they hadn't sat with Zach through measles and pneumonia. Their interest couldn't possibly be as intense as mine and a party is a party.

By 3:00 we were into jeans and on the street with R. and M., a happy five exploring the Arab markets and then climbing six miles to the highest point above Jerusalem, above the Necropolis to look back and across to Jerusalem the Golden, now grey, green and rose in the diminishing light.

We climbed a narrow, paved, winding path set between high

stone walls, and a man sitting astride a donkey and driving a foal on a rope approached and then overtook us, climbing the limestone stairs at the top with his soft-furred, good-willed beasts. Then he disappeared across the horizon.

Paul approached a gap in a small stone building set into a hill, climbed down three steps to peer into the darkness and then pulled back as a bat soft-blacked its way out and into the evening.

We climbed up until there was no Jerusalem left and there at the top at the Arab Intercontinental Hotel found hot chocolate and a taxi back. The day couldn't have been fuller and much of it was wonderful: Zach, the light and Jerusalem.

December 22

Zach woke with an upset stomach, probably a combination of the excitement of the previous day and too much chocolate just before bed. So instead of coming with us to the Israel Museum this morning he decided to rest in his room. I'm sorry he didn't join us because the museum complex is extraordinary. The buildings sit on a hill of their own, built within the last twenty years, and some portions more recently. I looked in vain for a book documenting their construction. The sureness of the architect's hand speaks of the same confidence I've seen everywhere. It's irresistible and inclusive.

We looked through the museum too hurriedly and came away with little more than impressions. I'd like to know more about the collection, especially the contemporary Israeli work, and again was disappointed in not finding a comprehensive catalogue. The Billy Rose Sculpture Gardens rival those of the Maeght Foundation in Vence. In fact, the setting was so dazzling that in some instances it unfairly competed for attention with the work on display.

Paul and I returned to the hotel to collect Zach, who had rallied, and to meet our tour guide Avi with whom we spent the first day. This time the tour group would be my favourite company—just the three of us, and guide—in a car.

We drove to the Western Wall and then set out on foot. The tour started with the El Aqsa Mosque and then the Mosque of Omar, the Dome of the Rock, both built on Mount Moriah. Before we could enter the compound we had to give over our bags and parcels for a search. Then, to enter the mosques we had to leave bags, parcels *and* shoes at the gate. Standing barefoot on cold stone in this immense, domed, glittering and highly significant religious shrine is humbling. To the vulnerability we felt at standing without our shoes in this vast open space was added the edginess of being in an enclosure controlled by Jordanians. Soldiers patrolled continually, rifles in hand.

The tentative nature of security, the randomness of fanatic and terrorist activity, lend a bite to perception. Are you ever not wheeling around here? But there's something else operating. In spite of the ever-present dangers I'm finding an odd comfort and a strange security in being in a setting where *my* people are making the decisions. People with my sensibilities, my values, are in charge in Israel and it has induced a sense of well-being I haven't felt before. I'm surprised. I thought I was more thoroughly Canadian than that.

From the mosques we began to walk from the site of the trial of Jesus, whose name Christ, Avi told us, means anointed in the manner of preparation for all Jewish burials, along the Via Dolorosa, passing all fourteen stations, through the market-place to the Church of the Holy Sepulchre. The Church was constructed on Calvary Mountain in the seventh century and has undergone restorations until the present time. The violence of the imagery of the icons was astonishing, unlike Christian images I've seen anywhere as an art-history student or as a traveller looking at art. It surprised and troubled me. I thought, how inappropriate in a religion with a tradition of preaching and proselytizing not to use this important site as an opportunity to encourage harmony.

Our walk took us through the foodstuff portion of the market. As much as the religious iconography would provoke violence and reaffirm our nastiest mortality, so too would that portion of the market. What we do to stay alive! One market alcove sold goats' heads. In a row were trim and perfect, uniform, black-haired, disembodied goats' heads looking benign in death as they were in life and as gentle and pacific as the religious icons are not. Beside the haired heads were the smooth and shiny rubber-glove-coloured, cleansed heads, still benign and forgiving and ready for eating. Sitting in this John the Baptist menagerie was the barber/butcher shaving the head of a goat in transition. I've always thought of myself as a survivor but never with more distaste. While I don't immerse a goat's head into a kettle of boiling water, we humans do. Nice measure, this walking through the market. Nothing was heat-sealed or foil-wrapped here.

A lot about being in Israel is a searching for the source. In keeping with that quest we drove to the area of Jerusalem where the Jewish Zealots live, to buy a *tallis*. The district called Mea Shearim is populated by the ultra-orthodox, Chassidic Jews. Every man was wearing a black suit, some with long coats, all with the flat broad-brimmed hats. It was late in the day and the narrow streets were dark, the odd lighted store interior the only clue to the twentieth century. My inclination was to ensure protection for these unworldly, other-worldly people but they apparently don't need it and don't want it. They're aggressive, even militant about their beliefs, intolerant of those who live otherwise, stoning buses that pass nearby on the Sabbath, refusing to vote or even be registered, conducting themselves with the confidence that a direct voice to God gives them. And this State allows for and protects all these variations. Children in school today learn Hebrew, English and Arabic. Without discrimination all religious sites are protected and even maintained. My feelings—no one should tamper or interfere with this country. Whatever the source of the sense of rectitude, this People is right, I felt. Imagine, only three days in Israel and I'm convinced that a Plan exists!

December 23

Our party, Zach, Paul and I, father-in-law, stepmother-in-law, sister-in-law, brother-in-law, nieces, cousins, aunt and uncle, left Jerusalem early in the morning with a guide, all of us tucked into a mini-bus heading south into the occupied territory of Jordan. Our ultimate destination was Tel Aviv but we would take a side tour to the Dead Sea, stop overnight, visit Beer Sheva and arrive late the following day in Tel Aviv.

The West Bank is now in Israeli hands. As we approached Jericho we were required to pass through a check-point manned by machine-gun-carrying Israeli soldiers, one of whom was a woman. We entered the city of Jericho, the oldest city in the world, set in a tropical valley, amply supplied with water from the Spring of Elisha. This source provides sufficient water for the cultivation of banana plantations and every kind of exotic vegetation. The sweetest oranges are said to grow in this valley, which shimmers green, entirely surrounded by desert.

In the dusty grey and beige gullies and valleys of the desert surrounding Jericho are groups of tents and small corrals. The Bedouins with their herds of sheep and goats live here, scrabbling sustenance from the meagre vegetation around them.

Tending the flocks and driving them along are spare and weathered men and boys, sometimes astride a donkey, and dressed in flapping clothes which make them blend and disappear into the landscape. The sheep and goats are the colour of the sand and stone. There is no identifiable time reference and it struck me that survival might be tied to a person's ability to pass unnoticed through the ages. In this difficult and marginal geography if you could just slip by no one would come to claim you before your time had been spent.

The only trees around here are acacia, sturdy, squat and oriental. But the women in their long wraps are willows or reeds and I wonder where they learned that. They come into sight, walking with no apparent origin or destination, or you see them loading twigs onto a complacent donkey who stands to be burdened until he becomes a form of mobile vegetation. We bus by, our guide speaking to the twelve of us through unnecessary amplification, more out of time with our surroundings than these Bedouins and beasts.

We stopped for a short time in Jericho to drink a glass of fragrant tangerine juice and the fruit-stand owner handed me a sprig of jasmine. I tucked it into the window at my seat and its scent accompanied me for the whole of the trip. Just beyond the road we travelled lay the River Jordan. We couldn't cross or even approach it. But the Dead Sea was now visible and we could see Jordan's mountains across its luminous surface.

We stopped at Tumran, the settlement where the Dead Sea Scrolls were written, then wrapped in linen, sealed in clay jars and hidden in caves. Not a sprig of vegetation interrupted the space that fell in front of us. Standing on a wooden viewing platform we looked out across a vast dry gully. On its opposite side were the sandstone caves that hid the scrolls for so many centuries. The young goatherd who found the treasure-filled caves must have been himself as sure-footed as his little goats.

What an inhospitable location for civilization to begin. Maybe it was a test. How badly did we want to be a literate society, making choices and plans? Badly enough to reckon with intense heat, unyielding soil, rock and drought? Apparently. And badly enough to believe that since this was where it began, this is where it should endure.

We drove on. This dry and contentious piece of land which everyone wants is now beginning to be made green and productive. The Israelis train Jordanian farmers in the most sophisticated agricultural techniques, teaching them about irrigation and soil nourishment. Once they've been trained, instead of staying on in the occupied West Bank to work, the trainees return to Jordan, taking with them their newly gained knowledge. In Jordan they put all these techniques to use and plant their own crops along the borders. Now they have a stake in ongoing peaceful relations and they refuse to allow terrorists access to strike out against Israel from their now greened land.

Our next stop was Massada.

I have been interested in Massada since excavations began there in earnest in the late '60s. It has a special significance for contemporary Israelis who vow that Massada will never happen again—no more surrender, no more defeat, no more capitulation. I had grown up hearing these kinds of stories and thrilled at all of that.

Our bus pulled into the parking lot. We walked up to a paved courtyard where the aerial tramway waited. We were discouraged from climbing the Snake Path on foot. Everyone opted for the cable car. The alternate way wasn't marked or indicated in the courtyard but it was possible to buy guidebooks, sandwiches, soft drinks and bottled water.

I loathe cable cars. They terrify me and if I'm going to the plateau of Massada as a witness, I'll not be spirited up on oiled bearings. Instead I'll grit and scrap and scramble my way up.

My father-in-law and Irene had a full agenda planned, which included a survey of Massada and then arrival at the Moriah Springs Hotel in time to bob in the Dead Sea. It takes a full forty-five minutes to climb to the plateau by foot. I was being a nuisance. Paul, bless him, recognized the set of my jaw and volunteered to accompany me. Sandwiches in hand, bottled water for a toast at the summit, we set out. Since the recommended mode is tramway, the Snake Path has not been maintained. Sliding rock and weather have made it invisible in some places but up was the only way and that limited our route choices. To say it didn't look as far up as it was would be untrue. It loomed, it was formidable. After all, the Romans surrounded and laid siege to Massada for eight months, unable to gain entry, and nothing significant has been done to make the plateau more accessible.

The rock rises 1424 feet above the Dead Sea so we climbed. Slipping stones, no railings, a direct not gradual ascent, the walls of the mountain sheared off, which was why it had been a natural site for a fortress. We had to rest often. My heart beat so quickly it seemed to seek exit from my chest. I pressed my hand hard against my chest to slow it down. We had to hurry because the others, who had taken the cable car up, were touring with our guide and were anxious for immersion in the Dead Sea.

I'm afraid of heights. I remember the terror of the pyramids in Mexico. I'll fall directly off or be paralysed by panic and be unable to move up or down. But I climbed, staring hard at the rock-face. The last forty feet were real stairs cut in the rock. A shed housed an attendant taking tickets. "Me pay! Are you mad! Serve me champagne instead!" But he wasn't only a guard, he was an Israeli with white teeth and he laughed and said he would if he could and then we stepped out onto the plateau. The cramped fear flew from me and was swept off by the wind. I won't forget or easily repeat the sight of the world up there, a separate country fit for King Herod and after him fit for defending to the death as the Zealots did.

The structures Herod built for himself were appropriate to his legend. It's hard to believe that a man of his vision really did exist. Today he would have to be no less than a corporate conglomerate. Then, he was a man never diminished by scale who surrounded himself with a luxury which reflected that. Decorated rooms standing on raised floors under which flowed hot air so that the room could be heated. Baths with mosaic floors and frescoed walls painted to simulate marble pillars in the Greek style, a series of circular terraces on the cooler north side for use in the summer, a swimming pool at the top of a 1000-foot-high plateau open to desert evaporation and kept filled. A man to reckon with.

After Herod, the Zealots sought isolation and safety there. The beauty of Herod's palaces were of little moment. Preservation of a way of life and then of life itself was their intent until they decided that survival at any cost was too costly. Nine hundred and sixty-seven people with storehouses and cisterns well stocked chose ten men to kill them, saving them from the sin of suicide, then one of the ten killed the remaining nine and then himself. They wouldn't be slaves, they wouldn't yield. Israelis vow there will never be another Massada.

The descent was easier but probably more dangerous. Giddy and exhilarated after toasting each other with bottled water, we slid and jogged down in ten minutes. Into the bus and off to the Dead Sea spa.

It's a comfort to know that so many people find relief from a variety of ills in its waters but to me it appeared malevolent, other-worldly, but *not* celestial. Its luminous green-blue changed to pink nacre as the sun set, and then to grey. It supports no life—no vegetation or sea creatures. There's no tide, no movement, just pads of salt pushed to the surface here and there. A few hotels hover at the shore, more clinic than vacation spot. Meals are served at a set time and choices are limited. There are two dining-rooms, milk or meat. Service is cheery. I haven't had even passably good wine in Israel and something about the food is depressing. With the odd exception it's somewhat dull, as if attention to the stomach beyond basic nourishment is too trivial to consider. One dish tonight, surprisingly tasty, calves' brains and scrambled eggs, leads me to look forward to grassy green dreams—a contrast to today's landscape. I find this spa unnerving and eerie. Nothing would induce me to attend voluntarily and I look forward to the 8:00 a.m. departure tomorrow.

Irene loves the Dead Sea, and spas, and comes here annually. She told me that five years ago when you looked across to Jordan at night there was only blackness. Now there are points of light indicating active settlements, but I miss my verdant prairies.

December 24

Tel Aviv—a major city, a metropolis on the Mediterranean. Ten p.m. and we've returned to our room after an excellent meal eaten in a small restaurant on the street which runs along the sea.

Understandably, beef and veal are luxury items in a country struggling to reclaim itself from the desert. Poultry is easier and more economical to raise but there are only so many ways to serve chicken. In North America we're accustomed to schnitzel being veal and to our surprise and delight, tonight it was. Green beans with almonds and for dessert a flaky pastry with whipped cream. Tel Aviv is a more secular city than Jerusalem, where mixing milk and meat at a single meal hadn't happened. It was a daring culinary combination but one we're accustomed to at home. The three of us ate our meal alone, and I ordered a carafe of white wine, the first good wine since we've been here, and I toasted and drank. I'm feeling slightly unfocussed but that's more a result of the unbearable day we spent than of the wine consumed.

I knew from the beginning that this trip would be paid for and I had a pretty fair measure of the currency of exchange. Today was the day the banker called our loans and no one rode in to save us—no white horses, no white hats. But why should there have been—we knew the facts before we entered the bargain, didn't we? So today came as no surprise. It was long and difficult, but no surprise. A regular day—blue sky, bags down early, everyone onto the bus. Now on the bus, my father-in-law took over the microphone. We set out for Sede Boger where David Ben Gurion began to turn the desert green as it had been long before. We were met at the experimental station, an oasis now, impressive, progressive and green, by a Bostonian professor turned zealot who spoke passionately and intelligently about what David Ben Gurion's vision and practice had been. He turned us over to another American professor who turned us over to an Israeli woman who guided us through the rest of the day. Ahava was a woman in her early thirties.

She was expecting her second child in four months. It would be difficult to imagine how many hundreds of North American tourists she talked to in a year but her pleasure in instructing and explaining seemed real. She wasn't working for a tour company. She was living here and she wanted us to understand what the people were doing, what the long-term goals were and what made up the small victories. None of the guides represented "big business." The statistics we heard from her and others throughout the trip had nothing to do with gross national product or return on investment. The triumphs had to do with tomatoes in the desert, desalination of water for gardens, growing edible sea kelp in small tanks of waste water, and children and refugees in schools. The achievements are awesome, the vision commendable and overwhelming but attainable, the example something one can't help but fall short of. Nothing less than *Aliyah* is good enough. As a substitute (you see I have a life, a family and a commitment to another country as well) I can send money, which is never enough. The abiding feeling is guilt and inadequacy. Powerful motivating factors, those, and at the same time unassuaged. That too is part of the transaction. What do I owe in exchange?

I'm impatient, intemperate and tired. I work hard and I'm stingy with my leisure time. With the exception of our short visit to Ben Gurion's kibbutz, this was a wasted day. But the time this day filled can be stretched and drawn to fill a lifetime. In boredom alone.

Another thing. I've never liked power. I don't like the people who have it, don't trust the people who seek it. In small things or large it never works fairly. People get bullied. They lose their voice. Their needs aren't met. Too much is given over to satisfy the people who are pressed to accumulate it. In the closed intimacy of our mini-bus, in the gather of our group, in a manner almost, but not really, benign, I watched it working today.

From Sede Boger we drove to Beer Sheva, to the Ben Gurion University of the Negev. We met for lunch in a cold room set aside for visiting donors. The president, his assistant and other officials joined us for lunch. Tables in the shape of a T were set. We sat down. My father-in-law rearranged us. The president sat in the middle of the T. Zach sat next to him. Paul and I were assigned flanking positions. Paul's father sat next to me. He assigned the reluctant Irene the place next to Paul. That left the two end places. R. and his friend sat there. The rest were left to sit as they were.

A speech by the president, surely there must have been something more important for him to do, a decent lunch anxiously served, a long speech by my father-in-law. He stood—a short, stocky man—and he spoke, working each word in his mouth like a hard fruit candy before releasing it. He introduced everyone around the table. Anyone with a title beyond his Christian and family name was identified with sufficient detail to satisfy *Burke's Peerage*.

As I sat shivering in the chilly room, I thought, who is he talking to? Most of us here are family and have been together without a break for almost a week—all seeing the same things, receiving the same information. The others around the table are Israelis. They live here. What is there to tell them?

Then he called on Zach to stand and speak. I whispered to him, "You're embarrassing Zach," so he called on Paul who speaks often and well and confidently, and then he called on me, and I spoke. I sat, saying I didn't need to stand since I was among friends, and I talked briefly, very briefly about the courage and tenacity and rightness of the Israeli people and about the emotional impact witnessing all of this was having and I thanked the Israelis for being in Israel and I hated my father-in-law.

More was still to come. My father-in-law is a lawyer and well known throughout Canada. In Israel and in the Jewish community at home he is regarded as a major financial donor and as effective counsel but now he had us participating in a day where I felt increasingly uncomfortable. The power which has me so uneasy continued to assert itself. Several people devoted their day to attend us. We were shown the library of the Medical School by the chief librarian, who also must have had other things to do. We were invited to view the emergency facilities of the hospital and were accompanied by a hospital official. Then to City Hall where a councillor and the deputy mayor greeted us in a building emptied of employees. The deputy mayor showed us around, providing a forum for Paul's father to display his knowledge of Beer Sheva municipal politics, information he received the last time he attended some official function there. We were served coffee and the children were presented with souvenirs. The deputy mayor is a research scientist as well as an elected city official. He is married and has children. His day begins early and by 4:00 he can count on being free. At 4:00 today a bus full of North Americans drew up to the municipal buildings and he was trapped. I was trapped. My poor sister-in-law, who trips everywhere photographing my father-in-law, was trapped.

We left Beer Sheva at 5:00 and arrived in Tel Aviv at 7:00. Our hotel is close to the Mediterranean and I can hear the sea and it's not trapped. So tonight I'll turn up the heat for Paul who is always cold at night and I'll open the patio doors and I'll sleep with the sea in my ears and I won't be trapped anymore. I'll think of grey fur and a cold black nose and loud and stubborn exchanges with good friends at home and the way my heart races and I won't be trapped.

December 25

Everything has been rearranged. Imagine December 25th not being Christmas! It was a luxury not to bend or even acknowledge someone else's form. The sense of sanctuary is everywhere. That's what Israel is about this second time around. Since 1948 Jews have had a voice, a place not only to run to but a place where they're welcomed.

Nonetheless, while I feel at home here, this is not in fact my home and I'm finding the travel tiring and difficult. There's a certain aimlessness and I miss a focus and an opportunity for assessment. There's no one here willing to enter into it with me.

This morning we walked with my aunt and uncle along the Herbert Samuel Esplanade. It's a patterned brick-inlaid walk which curves along the Mediterranean and we followed it all the way into Old Yafo where we were to meet the others for lunch. In one of the artisans' shops I bought a pair of earrings, pink mother-of-pearl, the colour of Jerusalem, set in silver.

We were invited to eat at the home of an Israeli friend of my father-in-law and Irene. Her apartment was in the old city, in a small townhouse complex reserved for artists. Set on a series of levels each opening to a stone patio overlooking the sea, it was a charming location and she entertained in a simple and pleasant manner. Lunch was plain and very tasty—a thick vegetable soup, chunks of fresh bread, salad and a chocolate cake made especially for Zach.

After lunch we walked and poked along the route to the hotel and beyond, venturing onto Dizengoff Street, the main shopping area of Tel Aviv. The street is given over to pedestrians and by 4:00 was crowded. There were record shops, grocery stores, bookstores, clothing stores—the kinds of shops you'd expect to find on any commercial street—but the largest number of businesses were restaurants and snack bars, places where people could gather to visit. More social than commercial, the street seemed an occasion for partying rather than shopping and indeed little attention was given to merchandising. Window displays and the contents offered were lack-lustre and out of date and no effort was made to capture the teen-age market which makes up such a large percentage of North American sales. I was reminded that Israel's focus is more basic than ours—survival is still the first issue.

The rest of the group had plans for the evening so Paul and Zach and I continued to pad and poke, buying foodstuffs for breakfast since our hotel suite has a little kitchen and then lying down in our rooms for what was supposed to be a short nap.

Three hours later we awoke to find a rain-filled night and the hour too late for dinner. We had a small snack in the hotel coffee shop and returned to our rooms. Zach is asleep in his bed, and, as on each night of this trip, I am writing down the day accompanied by intermittent snores from Paul.

I've learned that travelling in a group is something I'll never do again and that in most cases it seems I travel alone wherever I go anyway.

December 26

We slept late this morning, not waking until 9:00—no tour buses to catch—breakfasting lazily from the stores bought the night before and then venturing forth in a somewhat reluctant and perfunctory way into a rainy Tel Aviv morning to the campus of the university where the Museum of the Diaspora is located. The campus is glorious—large, creatively designed concrete buildings surrounded by rose gardens. We must see this museum, everyone said. So we did and came away confused. It seemed the same story was being told over and over. Maybe that is the whole story—struggle, wandering, survival, resettlement, struggle. And maybe the story was set to be told to outsiders, to people who hadn't grown up with it. But our sense was that the displays, while clever and beautifully presented, became redundant and the line between educating and proselytizing began to blur. Proselytizing has never been part of our tradition. Why start now? Or who was the museum designed for? We tired of the repetition of display techniques before we had worked our way through the three floors and left without seeing it all in detail.

Back into a taxi. Until Israel, part of the appeal of travel was the anonymity you had in moving through a place where you didn't know anyone. In Israel the feeling is that you know everyone or at least have seen everyone at the home of a relative on some occasion or other. The obverse is that everyone knows you and everyone has an opinion to offer, whatever the topic. It's often funny and I'm enjoying it.

By way of chit-chat and for information I asked the taxi driver if there were any place I might rent a horse and take a ride along the sea. Suddenly it was as if the driver had been in touch with my mother. "What do you want to ride for? Why look for trouble?" I assured him I was a skilled rider with a horse of my own at home. "You don't know Israeli horses. They're wild," he countered. I told him mine was a Thoroughbred and very spirited. I felt I could handle an Israeli pleasure hack. "Do you know any Israeli horses? How many

Israeli horses do you know?" he pressed. Well, he had me there. I had to confess I had no personal knowledge of any and let it go. We asked him to take us to the market area and he drove us to the Carmel Market where we walked through block after block of bazaar-style clothing shops and household goods until we reached the foodstuffs area.

The day had been cloudy with intermittent rain. As we moved through the closely built, stone alley-ways of food stalls, rain came down in pointing fingers, ribbons, strings, all the measures of the market. And everyone began to chant and clap "*Mayim, mayim*" (water, water). Gratitude for water everywhere. The sun was low and while the rain came down it held its position and lighted on a mound of tangerines still wearing green-leaved wings.

I want to have a small apartment here. In it I'll prepare red peppers, orange squashes; for it I'll choose from shining mounds of oily green and black olives, from pyramids of persimmons, dates, apricots, almonds, fishes, the whitest cauliflowers, over-sized magenta radishes, small fragrant bananas, full purple eggplants, sweet tomatoes, goat cheeses with surfaces scratched into patterns, and life-sustaining breads. There I'll bring tightly curled roses, black-powder-centred anemones and fragrant coffees.

Each thing I put into my wicker basket will carry with it the singing, insistent, ageless voice of its vendor. I'll carry the market into my rooms on my shoe bottoms—leaf residue, tobacco spit, animal offal, footprints and rain. I'll augment my careful wardrobe with a silver-threaded neck scarf, I'll wrap my hair in a black-gone-rusty head shawl, I'll replace my dressed leather boots with rubber ones. I'll peel vegetables on an outdoor balcony, coloured plastic clothes-pegs will materialize and attach themselves to pieces of fabric whose use is unidentifiable and I'll sing and caw in a new voice.

Here I'm surrounded by benedictions. I know Hebrew only as a language of prayer and blessings. In the market especially, but everywhere, people are speaking to me from the Bible. "Buy my fresh bread, hot chickpeas, avocados, salamis, amen." My sense is that their sense is that each utterance *is* a prayer. So I walked through the market, in the rain, with debris clinging to my boots and with a smile on my face.

Where was my Caravaggio to paint this beatification? He would know that this may be as honest as the Ecstasy of Saint Theresa and easier to achieve too. I also have before me the possibility of further ecstasies—which I'll seize. Witnessing stacked avocados only makes me greedier.

This evening an excellent fish dinner with R. and M. After the meal Zach and R. took off in search of some serious jazz. Paul and M. and I walked back along the sea and finished the day with a brandy in the hotel's lounge.

December 27

Today was the day for travel out of Tel Aviv. We rented a car and invited my aunt to join us. We headed north along the sea to Netanya, a resort town, modern and not terribly interesting. The next stop was Caesarea, first a Roman town built on a beautiful natural bay and later a Crusader battlement and city, and finally, abandoned to ruin. The amphitheatre has been restored. Concerts performed in full view of the sea would rival those performed at the Met or La Scala. Not much excavation has been done but the removal of earth reveals the accretion of one civilization on another and the disregard each had successively for the former. So elegant Doric marble columns lie horizontally, used as shoring for sub-basements. The intent of the archaeological project has not been made clear and the printed legends which would have been helpful were absent.

We drove on to Haifa. If God were to choose a contemporary industrial site for the delivery of another message, this would be it. It's Israel's major seaport, a bar of land into the sea, allowing the Mediterranean to be seen from two sides. At the same time most of the city is built on and between two rock mountains which are covered with both temperate Mediterranean vegetation and lush but controlled tropical flowering shrubs. It's an old city dating to the Byzantine period and earlier. In the late nineteenth century there was a wave of German immigration and the population has continued to grow. It's more prosperous than Tel Aviv and more European in character. Contemporary architecture is quite stunning, and apartments and villas are designed with terraces and balconies which give a hanging garden effect. The sea is visible unexpectedly through the trees, between buildings, at the base of cliffs and always very far below. The centre of the city is nineteenth-century, middle-class northern European with eastern food stalls scattered everywhere.

Since the day was Friday, people were making preparations for the Sabbath. It was a delight to be aware of it. Around 1:00 p.m. small flower stalls were set up, selling bouquets to be taken home for the Holy Day. By 4:00 p.m. all the shops were closed, the streets were free of traffic and in the orthodox section street barricades were set up to prevent the passage of any vehicles.

Everywhere fathers leading sons by the hand were rushing to synagogue. Everywhere men and boys wore *keepot*. This must be one of the reasons for Jews moving here—the feeling of being surrounded by your own, of being in a place where doing this is not only tolerated or protected as a multicultural oddity, but where celebrating in this way is the norm, codified as part of the civil law.

What a shock then to be returning on the Tel Aviv/Haifa highway at 5:00 with the car radio on. The English-language news from Jerusalem reported that this afternoon terrorists shot and killed thirteen people at the El Al counter at the Rome airport and three people at the El Al counter at the Vienna airport. We were chilled and silent. Here I've felt so safe, but in the world all over we're in such jeopardy. I don't understand, but somehow there's a tie with the strata of cultures we saw this morning at Caesarea. Everything turns and is turned on its end and the only thing that prevails is the hatred the world feels for the Jews. It's as enduring as the anonymous and nondescript shells lodged in the mortar between the stones of the Romans and the Crusaders.

This evening the group gathered for a last *Shabbat* dinner together before we all disperse. We ate at the Dan Hotel, the oldest on the sea strip in Tel Aviv, well built and secure. The dining-room is located below ground. I don't usually care for subterranean settings. This time it felt safe. The feeling around the table was subdued because of the news, because of the partings and because in some way we'd all let each other down. My impatience and intolerance will poison me yet but I can't be accused of failing to turn my critical eye inward, I just can't close it.

Paul toasted my father-in-law, thanking him for this Bar Mitzvah trip. He answered in a genuine and simple manner, everyone too tired for pomp and puffery. I know we all wish each other well. I wish myself to be better.

Tomorrow is our last day here. Until the news this afternoon I was looking forward to leaving. Tel Aviv in intermittent rain is not an irresistible city. Now I feel somehow that I should be staying not for safety but for identification and to stare the bastards down.

We've passed two *Shabbats* in Israel. On both occasions we took our Sabbath meal in the dining-rooms of the Dan Hotel, one in Jerusalem, one in Tel Aviv. I don't know just now if I much believe in a brotherhood of man. The newest edition of the *International Harold Tribune* gives us reason to doubt it exists. For now I'll narrow my grouping to include the nation of Jews. Here, on *Shabbat* with everyone in the dining-room, people from all over the world, saying prayers to welcome the Sabbath, prayers for the wine and for the bread, in different accents, in this context I feel very much a part of a large group. I'm an only child. I grew up accustomed to solitude. I developed, out of preference or necessity, a certain self-sufficiency. As an adult I've continued in this manner. The feeling of membership is novel, will undoubtedly diminish with distance from Israel. It was important to have felt this direct communion. I'll be able to come back to it now that I know it's here. Sabbath in Israel is not an ordinary day.

December 28

Our last day. We met R. and M. and set out for the Tel Aviv museum. It's a new building, with an attractive exterior set back in a large plaza filled with some good sculpture, flowering shrubs and roses. The inside is fine. Getting inside took some doing. R. and M. had tried late yesterday afternoon and were told that the gallery was closing but that it would be open on Saturday. We were surprised that anything would be open on Saturday, the Sabbath, but this is a country where you take everything on faith. People were queuing up and others were going directly inside. They had bought tickets yesterday before sundown, knowing that the gallery would not sell them on the Sabbath. However, those queuing up were buying tickets from a man who was not directly in the employ of the gallery but happened to have an unlimited supply. What a country!

The gallery has an interesting and varied permanent collection, a fine selection of Impressionist pieces, good international contemporary work as well as a large collection of Israeli paintings, both contemporary and as early as the '20s. Seeing only one or two paintings by an artist whose work you've never looked at before is tantalizing and frustrating and I've been unable to find good art books. Both here and at the Israel Museum in Jerusalem what I wanted was an Israeli art devotee to act as a guide. There has clearly been an active visual arts community here for some time and I wanted to know something about it.

We left the gallery after 2:00 tired and hungry and headed for Old Yafo for lunch by the sea, in the sun. We found a beautiful restaurant and had fish with garlic, wine and sunshine, chocolate mousse with toasted hazelnuts and big glasses of sweet strawberries topped with heavy cream. The dairy foods here rival those of Normandy. Coffee and good chat, then a long walk back along a wild sea to our hotel. The whole route winds along the Mediterranean and is paved mosaic-style with large coloured bricks. Rounded alcoves with stone benches line the way. In a country struggling to survive, where so much money must be spent on defense, on salvaging the land from the desert, on rebuilding what's been destroyed, on bringing civilization to people determined to resist it, how is there still enough for stone benches, public gardens and paved walkways along the sea?

In Canada, in the flourishing, over-nourished West, our leaders trip in their haste to give our parks and waterways over to the developers. With people in mind whom I value and hold dear, who are not Jewish, I've fought throughout the whole of my stay here against shouting out an exclusive and prideful response. On my last night in Israel I'll yield. There's money for stone benches and gardens and paved seaside walkways because here all these things really are valued. These are the choices that are made. The people in this country *are* special!

Tomorrow we face the rest of the world.

December 29

We were awakened on request at 4:00 a.m. Paul had taken our bags to El Al the previous night for an advance security check. Doing this allowed us to arrive at the Lod Airport one hour before departure instead of two. We met a road-block a half-mile outside the airport and soldiers stopped each vehicle and peered inside. At the airport were more soldiers. A pervading quiet attended there, on the plane, and throughout the journey, continuing at the baggage claim at Leonardo da Vinci Airport. The El Al flight landed in Rome without incident. The pilot's parting words to us were his thanks for our flying El Al and the wish that in 1986 air travel would be free of terrorist attacks.

Soldiers and plain-clothed security men formed a cordon around the plane and then around the bus which took us to the terminal. Two cars, each with four men inside, motored beside the bus to the terminal, which at the entry area was empty except for soldiers with machine-guns in hand. We stood surrounded by security people while we waited to claim our bags. I felt like a small alert bird wary for the safety of the occupants of my nest. My eyes darted around without rest until our taxi was on the auto route to Rome. Ours had most probably been the first El Al flight out of Israel and into Rome after the shooting there and the evidence of violence and damage were still visible.

It was unfortunate timing to arrive in Rome on a day when some festivity encourages the random lighting of firecrackers. All day explosions ricocheted off building walls, causing us to start and gasp. We returned to our rooms exhausted by tension and fright.

The city is full of police in cars, on foot, and all, because of the terrorist attack, conspicuously armed. We've just come from a country where the people, especially the young people, are handsome, vigorous and healthy looking. Their dress is of no moment. Fashion is a luxury which hasn't been achieved in Israel yet. Here in Rome, the people we saw on their Sunday outings are well heeled, heavy-set and over-dressed. On this first day, coming directly from Israel, the comparisons I find myself making are not favourable, so first impressions must be replaced with better impressions as Israel recedes from my consciousness.

The city, however, is another matter. We slept for two hours in the early evening. Other than that, we've been walking. The overriding sense I have is of the grandness of scale and vision. Roman buildings were imperial and the early Christian structures borrowed that scale. These people did see themselves as emperors who controlled and defined the world. Where else but from the gods could that notion of scale have derived? If genetics, eugenics and modern medicine are right, we're bigger by a significant amount than the Roman builders and I wondered at the vision that inspired and informed their achievements. I look forward to the coming days when I can walk inside these spaces and I'm hungry for Caravaggio. Today we passed a large, locked Rizzoli's bookstore. Tomorrow we'll return there and find the book which will lead us to the treasures.

From my earliest days as an art-history student, Caravaggio's paintings have served as a touchstone for me. He was a renegade and an outsider in his art and his life, and his independence and toughness were appealing. Constrained by the need to satisfy his patrons and operate within the parameters of accepted conventions, he nevertheless made paintings that were radical and new. The subjects were religious—recognizable parables and Biblical events—but what he really painted were the street people he lived with, the disenfranchised, unruly, unwashed poor people who lived in the half-lit, body-warmed spaces the demimonde always occupy.

I'd seen only reproductions of his work. Now I would have an opportunity to stand in front of the canvasses. The colours would be true. I'd finally have a real sense of their scale. I could actually stand where the painter had stood when he finished his work. I couldn't wait.

December 30

The Vatican Museum is Michelangelo's last laugh. Here is retribution for the diminished sight he suffered from painting the ceiling of the Sistine Chapel. A rainy day, thousands of people whose clothing released the damp accumulated en route, all filing endlessly toward the goal buried deep within a building shameful in its excess of material accumulation—the wealth of the papacy. Whatever happens in Europe after centuries, rot or mildew or fatigue, was present there. Plunder, purchase, room after room of unidentified cultural spoor, room after room of frescoed ceilings. Signs in five languages holding out promise of the Sistine Chapel. Finally, a room the size of a soccer field, viewers packed shoulder to shoulder, heads cricked back, staring at a ceiling Michelangelo didn't want to paint. But he was good, and he spoke his piece and it doesn't look like anything else anywhere in that museum. Religion of course is out of the question, was never posed as a question. The sole promise—a way out—please where's the exit?

The balance of the day up and down the chic avenues looking at goods in the rain. Paul and Zach each bought shoes. Faced with a surfeit of goods, I panic and can't buy anything. Rescue at Rizzoli's where I bought a magnificent book on Caravaggio, in Italian. His brush, however, spoke my language. The other major purchase today was a green Michelin guide which will tell me how to find the Caravaggios illuminating Rome.

I asked about the painter in two bookstores. The vendors spoke no English but with the name Caravaggio they paused, eyes registered recognition and pleasure, and off they went. Caravaggio is the closest I've come to home in a while.

December 31, New Year's Eve

Getting at Rome in the rain is difficult. Enjoying Rome in the rain as midnight approaches is a pleasure which eludes me. There's a New Year's Eve custom of exploding firecrackers—no colour, no light, it seems, just noise—in some cases the whine that must have preceded explosions of World War II bombs, in other cases just a gunshot with sound amplified by stone walls and cobbled streets. I feel as if we were under siege. It's clearly the vestige of a celebration with the key component missing. Somewhere the joy was left behind and no one went back to collect it. Perhaps my perceptions are clouded by over-large lunches, heavy weather, too much of everything for sale and the endless crowds. I must have my prairie space or live at the top of a building.

We had planned a New Year's Eve dinner at a restaurant recommended by our concierge. Zach, however, was struck down by lunch. We cancelled our dinner plans, tucked Zach in and walked. The streets were full of couples. We found ourselves at the Piazza di Spagna, the oldest people there. Teenagers from all over the world lounged on the steps and at the fountain drinking and pairing off. Since we were already a pair we moved on.

At the Piazza Venezia we found a funny, crowded bar where we ate a little meal and were regaled by the patrons who all performed the same ritual. They rushed in, threw back a tiny espresso, pushed a sweet bun into their mouth and rushed out, all at Charlie Chaplin speed.

It's midnight now, the noise has increased, provoking me to unlatch our outer shutters and lean out the double windows. In some distant squares it appears there are firecrackers of the kind we see on Victoria Day. The air is filled with the smell of gunpowder but there are no people—just the noise, and now and then a little coloured light. Sleep will be difficult tonight but not, alas, for Paul who is already there.

Caravaggio continues to be elusive. We arrived at Santa Maria del Popolo where there are two of his paintings: *The Conversion of St. Paul* and *The Crucifixion of St. Peter*. We had just approached the chapel where they hung when we were hurried out—12:30 closing, not to reopen until 4:00. The Borghese Museum which has several was closed too, we were told. The rain continued to make walking difficult.

We cabbed to Piazza Navona, which is one of the oldest piazzas in Rome, unusual because of its rectangular shape. At Christmas, stalls are built up and down its sides. These are filled with candy, toys and the components for creating Nativity scenes. Some of the miniature pieces are wonderful and while setting up a crèche in my home is not what I had in mind, I bought a terracotta donkey and cow, two celestial putti and a butcher's stall that looked exactly like the ones we saw in the Arab market in Jerusalem. The square is beautiful. Three fountains, one Bernini's *Fontana dei Fiumi*, and two others. There's a fine seventeenth-century cathedral and buildings, ochre and ombre, sit on wet black cobblestones.

Travelling through Israel and now here, I have repeatedly had a thought that appears in a visual way. There's a ribbon that runs continually through time. It began at the beginning, it carries on unbroken. Sometimes you're there when it runs past. I sensed it today. In the Piazza Navona, in the thin pale light of late afternoon, two Cavaliere on matched white Hungarian mounts stepped up and back through the crowds. The horses were cool, well-trained. They picked their way among the people, stepping high. I didn't see them appear but I heard the horses on the cobbles and there they were, two men, slender, soft-haired, distant-looking in blue capes, grey breeches with a magenta stripe on each leg. Following them by chance, I think, were two garbed nuns on foot—two perfect pairs out of time, in time, not tagged to time. If Caravaggio eluded me, if it rained all day, this redeemed it for me.

Tomorrow everything will be closed—an inhospitable day for travellers. Maybe the weather will offer a charity. We're ready for the sun.

January 1, 1986

I had no idea it was as simple as asking. We woke today to sunshine and I should remember what a non-urban being I am, how closely tied to the weather my moods are. Sunshine outside, and my energy and enthusiasm return. And since I'm asking and receiving I'll request health and peace and happiness too, for all the people who fall within my dominion.

We breakfasted late in the rooftop restaurant of our hotel. It's called The Forum because it sits in the midst of the Foro Romano which includes the Coliseum and covers an area of many city blocks. The view from our table over the still-blooming geraniums and out onto massive stone arches and columns is grand.

We've been frustrated so far in our attempts to see the Caravaggios. Endless false starts, early closings, buildings locked for renovations have me concerned that we might leave Rome without having had a proper look. To ensure at least one successful encounter we took a taxi directly to San Luigi dei Francesi. Although everything is closed on New Year's Day, the churches are not, and for us they're also museums. There, in a small chapel to the left of the chancel, there are three Caravaggios. St. Matthew's Chapel contains *The Calling of St. Matthew*, *St. Matthew and the Angel* and *The Martyrdom of St. Matthew*. I can't say more than that I wasn't disappointed and that the best reproductions can't meet or match standing there.

From San Luigi we walked to the Pantheon. Having just come from Israel where there is clear evidence of civilization having existed for thousands of years more than the 2000 our twentieth century implies, I find the idea of dating historical events as B.C. or A.D. curious. As if time had been created by Christians. A perfect example is the Pantheon. I'm standing at the centre of a temple built twenty-seven years before the beginning of the Christian measure of time, under a dome 142 feet high and 142 feet in diameter, made of a single slab of poured and coffered concrete, unsupported except around the periphery. In the centre of the dome is an opening, an oculus through which you see the sky race past. The beams on the porch had been covered in bronze plates. They are no longer there but they're still in Rome.

In the fourth century its function as a temple dedicated to the Roman gods was deemed inappropriate and it was closed. In the year 608 it was reopened as a church. Along with St. Martin de Bocherville near Rouen and St. Etienne in Caen, it remains one of the most moving buildings in which I've stood.

It was a short walk to the Piazza Navona, still filled with stalls, balloon sellers, people and today, the sun. Zach with his archer's eye won me four little bottles of Italian liqueur and then together he and Paul shot down a big bottle of Spumante which Zach gave to a man sunning himself on a bench.

We walked to a good lunch and then to St. Peter's Basilica. Bernini's colonnaded arms are embracing and grand, and Michelangelo's dome, magnificent. The interior is without question awe-inspiring and optimistic too. It's light, and while we didn't examine all the chapels in detail, the imagery appears much less directed to anguish, agony and retribution than Calvary Temple. Alas, Michelangelo's *Pieta* is behind glass. It needs hands sliding over it now and then. Maybe the custodians do that. But it's the warmest marble I've seen. Mary's hand gesture, wrist turned, palm up, is as despairing as any. Mothers know that gesture.

The bronze plates taken from the Pantheon but still in Rome? They were removed by Pope Urbain VIII and melted down to be used in Bernini's Baldaquin, the main altar in St. Peter's.

More walking, then a nap, and a taxi to the Via Veneto to eat. We opened the door to an absolutely exquisite Chinese dining-room and ate like kings.

January 2

No sun, no art. Villa Borghese with its Caravaggios was closed for repairs. It rained for most of the day. The temperature dropped so that damp, cranky people became cold, damp, cranky people. We wished ourselves away from here. We ate a bad lunch and were wretched. The sky cleared a little, the air warmed, we relented. We won't leave early. But our frustration is real and well founded—galleries closed, street time difficult because of the weather and everything very costly. Travelling is difficult. It ranks as one of my favourite things to do but it's difficult. Removed from your familiar setting, faced with a language through which you can't move with ease, operating at a tempo which doesn't coincide with what has become habit, hungry at odd times, looking at menus which seem to obscure simple meal choices, confounded by taps that open left not right, constantly translating currency—the same qualities that make travel the most enriching experience reduce your sense of competence and have you inclined, on occasion, to lean against a building on a street which isn't where you headed, and whimper like a fretful child.

But by the time we returned to our hotel we were feeling cheerier. We'd made some small purchases, brought the people at home a little closer by buying gifts for them, and had rallied once again. We had a lovely dinner, more than fair compensation for our bad lunch, and plan tomorrow to see the Galleria Nazionale d'Arte Moderna.

January 3

When we awakened the sun was shining—it would be a good day. The cobbles of Israel and Rome and all the rain had ruined my black leather boots. The plan was—a quick trip to the Via del Corso to buy an elegant pair I'd seen there and then on to the Galleria Nazionale d'Arte Moderna.

The custom here is to criss-cross the narrow streets anywhere at all. The cars stop or swerve and there are few traffic lights. Mostly it seems to work. We were walking along the Via del Corso when a window display across the street caught our attention. We set out to cross as we'd been doing. I was in the lead, Paul directly behind and Zach somewhere to my right. As I stepped off the curb I saw a motor scooter approaching. Zach was still on the sidewalk, having seen it. Paul carried on. I grabbed at his sleeve and called to him to watch. His thoughts were somewhere else and as I watched, what was inevitable seemed to happen in slow motion. He collided with the motor scooter and was thrown to the pavement. I sprang toward him and he immediately responded with "I'm O.K." The driver had fallen to the ground, his machine spinning out sideways. We slid over to the sidewalk, both of us looking at each other only for a second to acknowledge that something horrible and damaging happens just that quickly. Paul was all right except for a throbbing elbow which had been the first point to touch the road. We were shaky and unnerved. The driver wasn't hurt and Paul barely scuffed his jacket sleeve but museums and art seemed too removed for now.

Instead, we walked in the sun, chattering back and forth like a pair of jays at opposite sides of a garden until we were sufficiently reassured. Then we flew into an orgy of shopping, falling exhausted into our rooms at night. Tomorrow—art.

January 4

A dry day, some sun, but cold. We walked to San Pietro in Vincoli, built in the fifth century but altered substantially in the fifteenth and sixteenth centuries. In design and decoration it's much simpler than most of the cathedrals we've been viewing. We were looking for Michelangelo's *Moses* and there it sat, warm and confident and not very much like stone. The forcefulness, the sureness—no ambivalence. All of Michelangelo's pieces we've seen put a firm hand on your shoulder and turn you to look them full in the face. His *Moses* is glorious. He knew that a man assigned to lead an enslaved people out of Egypt had to be tough stuff. The arms and shoulders are not those of a man whose life has been devoted only to study and contemplation. This was clearly a man who could lead and direct. The face, the brow—an intelligent but accessible being—probably lusty too. Someone real was the model for that piece.

From there to Santa Maria Maggiore, whose proportions are much grander. It's an enormous basilica begun in the fifth century with additions and alterations made from the twelfth century to the eighteenth. The mosaics in the nave and chancel were what we came to see and they are splendid, glittering, vivid and jewel-bright. They date from the fifth century and could rank with those in Ravenna.

From Santa Maria Maggiore we sought other spiritual nourishment. We bought tickets for the opera. Opera in Italy! I expect no less than everyone singing along. And since we were on the Via del Corso looking for exactly the shirt Zach had in mind, we crossed the Piazza del Popolo which lies at the end of del Corso to look again at the Caravaggios in Santa Maria del Popolo.

The church is a Renaissance building full of art treasures. In the Cerasi Chapel two Caravaggios: *The Conversion of St. Paul* and *The Martyrdom of St. Peter*. The paintings are large, over eight feet high. Dark private spaces, undisclosed light sources and the sense of a secret not fully revealed. Both figures, St. Peter and St. Paul, had been upended, thrown off balance, made vulnerable. The picture plane is uncertain, making the viewer's stance uncertain too. Unbalanced, you're drawn into the half light of the painting. Caravaggio, without creating an illusory three-dimensional space, had established a real place, a location that bears testimony to event, to anguish, pain and, above all, to sense.

As an art-history student my introduction to his work had been through the medium of slide transparencies. From there I searched out reproductions in books. I was hooked and determined to see them in the flesh.

Two years earlier Paul and Zach and I had travelled to Venice—of course to see the city and to attend the Biennale but my personal agenda had been something else. That wonderful opalescent city is near the city of Ravenna and I had to see the Byzantine mosaics there. Venice was engaging and seductive beyond anything I would have expected but at the outset it represented a place near a place I had to see.

Now, in Rome, there was a similar compulsion. I was interested in everything but here I would find Caravaggio. And finally, finally I was standing in front of two of his paintings. I was giddy. My eyes felt hot. It was hard to stand still. "Here they are. Here they are," was all I could say.

We fumbled for silver and fed the light machine. Thirty seconds passed and the lights clicked off. More change and then again the drama of revelation. It was almost better this way. It corresponded with Caravaggio's own attitude to light. When we'd run out of change, when I'd had my fill, we left.

We returned to the hotel late, ate out even later and walked back tired, well after midnight with Saturday-night Rome still pulsing and surging around us.

January 5

Our last day in Rome. Tomorrow noon we leave for Canada. This trip has been so foreign, so varied and filled with occasion for emotion that I feel we've been away for months. In distance we've touched three continents and are already beginning to lose reference points. I look forward to holding the beings I love and to finding my place once again. My place must include some solitude. That and tolerance are my resolve for the new year.

Today was sunny but cool. At the recommendation of the concierge we set out for the flea market. We found it mobbed and crowded with shabby and uninteresting new goods. We got out as quickly as the crowd would allow.

With the erratic opening and closing times of churches and museums, we didn't have enough time left to attend either, so we wandered and wondered at the colour of Rome and then set to our last grand lunch. These enormous meals in the middle of the day leave us sullen and slow. To my mind it's an entirely dysfunctional tradition. I'd recommend against it. Alas, the alternative is pushing down something doughy at a stand-up bar. The appeal of eating or drinking standing up escapes me but here it seems to be the mode. It's especially hard to understand in the context of the 1:00 to 3:00 p.m. closings everywhere, since people can't be saving their lunch hours for shopping or gallery gazing.

We returned to our hotel, gussied ourselves up and went off to the opera, *L'Elisir d'Amore* at the Teatro dell Opera di Roma. We had a box, private, discreet, a perfect place for an assignation but not for visibility, especially since we shared it with three people from Japan who understood everything but the suggestion that the chairs be arranged so that we all could see. That small irritation aside, the opera house was perfect. The orchestra area is smaller than North American concert halls, and with tier upon tier of blue velvet-lined boxes, gilt, crystal and rustlings. I loved it. Costumes, sets, lighting, choreography, voices—all were first-rate. There's an ease here. It is, after all, a language used in conversation and not just for performance. Opera is an affirmation and a celebration of some of what's best and the performance was presented with a confidence that made us believe it was even better than any of the operas we'd seen at the Met. And this isn't Italy's best opera company. It's just that opera is at home here.

It was dark when we left the theatre and we wanted to walk. There can't be anything more satisfying than walking these beautiful pink and ochre streets, crowded, lighted, and with daytime noise somewhat subdued. We wandered and came by chance upon the Trevi Fountain. The promise is that if you toss a coin into the waters you'll return to Rome some day. So we all did and it was the right way to end our stay here, better still because it happened by chance.

Tomorrow, my dear Canadians.

To Moscow, Odessa, Leningrad 1987

March 1, 1987

I've been invited to this place, this page, by a hotel room desk. At home when I write, I can only write in my study, with an arrangement of my things around me. My actual approach to the work is crab-like and sideways, avoiding the forward movement which would require that I come to the desk, pull out the chair, sit and write. But here, in a hotel room in Amsterdam, the invitation is direct and simple, take it or leave it. You've gone somewhere, unrolled miles behind you, travel interests you—write it down.

The last major trip I took was just over a year ago in circumstances as different from the present ones as reality can allow. Then, my family travelled to Israel to celebrate my son's Bar Mitzvah in Jerusalem. There was some tension, I'd been working hard and was preoccupied. Zach had had to do a lot of studying to prepare his *Mafter* and Paul had been growing increasingly distant and withdrawn. I should have taken note, should have stopped and tried to check the slide. But the things that signal a relationship's breaking down aren't epiphanic. It's only when the fabric has become worn and thin and transparent that you're able to see through it and at the same time look back at how it was when it was whole cloth. Then it's usually too late.

There were things, simple by themselves, not portentious. Something small but odd like evenings in our hotel in Rome. We'd return at the end of a day. Zach would plug in his earphones, listen to tapes, read and be a teenager. I'd sit at the desk and record the day or lie on the bed and read. Paul would lie back against his pillows and watch television. But it was Italian and he doesn't speak a language other than English so he'd watch pictures. Any program was okay. At the time it made me impatient. Thinking about it now, it just seems lonely, isolated, and I'm sorry.

For the most part, in Israel I'd set worry to the back and allowed myself to be drawn through heart and sense into a country I'll now always think of as home. Home in the sense of everything beginning there, home in the sense of refuge and sanctuary, home in terms of a singleness of purpose you probably only feel before leaving home.

Italy followed Israel and our flight to Rome followed immediately upon terrorist attacks at the El Al counters at the Rome airport. I had anticipated Rome as a glut for the eye in search of art, in particular the paintings of Caravaggio, and I had expected to find the light of Florence, Venice. The time was wrong, the streets were filled with armed patrols, the weather was cold, our time was wrong.

Once we returned home my marriage began disassembling itself, inexorably as though on a proscenium stage and I couldn't cross the orchestra to alter it. The footlights blinded me, the new script wasn't available to me, the director was out of control, was mad.

Paul had always talked about an individual's putting on a mask and then finding after a time that the mask couldn't be pulled from the face, had become the face. So there he was, a caricature for Punch. My life had become theatre and has so remained.

The legal term "living separate and apart" is more apt than jurists know. You are apart—in pieces, in fact—and the parts of your life become separated. There's no whole. A new centre must be found. I'm doing that. It's a journey—travel through an internal landscape as foreign and unknown as the destination we've set out for—Russia.

Evelyn Hart, the Royal Winnipeg Ballet's Evelyn Hart, has been invited to dance in Odessa and then at a gala concert in Moscow staged for her, partnered by one of the Bolshoi's leading dancers.

A film-maker from Toronto will turn the event into a movie. Winnipeg's "24 Hours" will produce a documentary on it. Robert Enright will do that and I'm with Robert and I'll write. Write and distance myself for a while from the endless emotional assaults at home, look to my interior landscape, lay it across a new one, the grid on a map, and read it.

It's an impossible thing to do—decide that in less than two weeks you'll travel to Russia. Everyone recommended against it. Fodor says no in 1987. Give yourself six weeks. It's not the sort of place for spontaneity. The travel agency in Winnipeg which provides the thin links between eastern bloc émigrés and their homeland said, "Impossible." Toronto's expert travel agency for Russia said, "No time." But this was the time. I found the real expert in Ottawa, a travel agent who said yes, who transferred, instructed, telexed, cleared and produced hotel accommodations and visa without problems and in time.

Departure at 1:15. One bag and a piece of hand luggage. Toronto is fog-bound and we circle and as we circle it becomes impossible to have our bags transferred to the connecting flight to Amsterdam. The night and day we have in Amsterdam before we leave for Russia may allow time for our bags to catch up with us. Two of the dancers from the Royal Winnipeg Ballet who will dance with Evelyn in Moscow are travelling with us. The costumes are in their luggage. Robert has bought new clothes for the filming. I have clothes in my suitcase for which I have a genuine fondness. If the bags are not going to make it, will we have time in Amsterdam to reassemble wardrobes for two weeks in Moscow? Is there insurance? Who pays? Who cares? Certainly not the airline.

We leave Toronto on a fully booked airplane, smokers on board. We're told to wait in the Amsterdam airport. A Canadian Pacific flight is crossing the Atlantic just after ours and may be carrying our bags.

Around and over the seat in front of me I can see the in-flight movie. *Peggy Sue Got Married.* Distilled American culture on a Dutch airline en route to Moscow. Cognitive dissonance becomes the norm.

March 2

The Amsterdam airport is clean, light, efficient. We file our missing baggage claims, have coffee and wait for the Canadian Pacific flight. Our bags are on it. We claim them, load them into a van and drive into Amsterdam.

Ahead of me is two weeks without the telephone. No one can say a litigious word to me. I've run off to the Soviet Union, escaped behind the Iron Curtain for a rest, for peace, and for two weeks have drawn it shut behind me.

A sandwich, a shower and then Robert and I take a taxi to the Stedlijk Museum. We have only a short time before closing and we look at the retrospective of a Dutch painter and photographer named Lucebert. Obviously significant in the Netherlands, clearly influenced by the work of major twentieth-century American and European painters, but with a quirky and disturbing, relentless sensibility of his own. It appears neither his style nor subjects have been much altered by the years. He holds to a vision that speaks of betrayal, isolation and leave-taking—geographic departures and departures from convention. There was one painting that haunts me still—the subject, the eternally conjugal and volatile Punch and Judy. Turtle-like we carry home with us no matter where we travel.

March 3

Robert and I ate an excellent Indonesian meal, talked about what we had seen and what we were about to see. After, we walked in the cold rain-snow until we were too cold to continue on foot. But the pleasure we felt at being in Amsterdam full of good food, double scotches, art, and each other's company made us skip and silly until we caught a taxi at the American Hotel and went home.

The night was an odd one. I had frightened myself with writing about Paul and the malicious unravelling of our marriage. Then the time change took sleep from me and when it did come I wakened two or three times with a start, anxious about entering Russia, me who likes to be in control wherever I am and have experienced so little of it lately.

We left Amsterdam at 11:00 a.m. The Amsterdam airport is about comfort and purchase, travel of course, but once past the ticket gates there's at least a quarter of a mile of shops selling luxury goods and specialty food, flowers, electronic equipment and I don't know what else. The shops are arranged along both sides of the corridors which lead to the gate from which we exited to the Soviet Union. We bought nothing, we weren't tempted, we didn't look back, we didn't become salt.

It was a small KLM plane and it wasn't full. We travelled just under two hours and landed in Warsaw. No one got on, most got off. Fourteen of us remained on board. Armed soldiers walked around the plane, in the cold, circling while the wind blew snow at their feet. For forty-five minutes we waited, they circled. We joked quietly among ourselves and felt some unease. Too late to reconsider, but anyway by now any edginess I'd felt earlier had been replaced by curiosity and I knew I'd have no problems with this trip. No terrain could be as foreign or as hostile as the one I'd been travelling at home for the past year. Here the signs would be in Russian.

Someone would understand them. My interior life, the life that's being dismantled, has no signposts at all.

As the plane lowered over Moscow it was night. The wings' lights illuminated a snowstorm, driven in part by the speed with which we were meeting it. The snow became attenuated lines, spinning, whirling bobbins in a textile mill, silkworms in a frenzy, snowstorm over Moscow.

An Aeroflot fleet of planes and a runway drifted over, dots of blue showing through the drifts to outline the route. Then a small car with flashing roof-lights appeared and signalled our plane to follow it in, our airship hauled along, the *Queen Mary* led by a tug into harbour.

I've been thinking a lot about landscape, in and out. In North America we're bound by our inherited European sensibility to tame and tend. We're at odds with our wild country. Nature was the enemy. It was necessary to beat it and bind it Christo-like, shrink it to our reckoning.

The Warsaw and Moscow airports let the snow drift in. Probably it's dangerous but I liked it. The fastidiously scraped and whisked runways at home are improbable for the prairies in winter.

March 6

Out of sequence. Time is rearranged, restructured here. It probably happened in 1917 when the whole country turned and turned again. So I'll write on Friday about Friday and then go back to find Tuesday. Or maybe it would be clearer to acknowledge that it's Friday and here I sit in the stadium-sized foyer of the Kosmos Hotel in Moscow, wondering at where I find myself and that an amazingly broad cross-section of the world is milling around my seat. If Russia is a closed country then certainly much of the world has managed to slip in: India, Africa, the Arab nations, Germany, Japan, France, America, Latin America, Canada, Soviet bloc countries.

There's a rhythm, a tide to the emptying and filling of the hotel lobby. Sometimes, but not often, it's empty of people. Sometimes it's like the lobby of any large hotel with people entering and leaving. But most often it's filled almost to the point of immobility by clots of people being organized to leave on tours or with groups registering or checking out.

In keeping with this country's political attitude, individuals have a dubious status. There's a stated and restated preference for groups and incredulity greets me each time I indicate I'm here as an individual and not with a group. "Alone, you're alone, not with a group, let me ask it again," giving me a chance to change my mind. "You're not with a tour group, you're on your own?" If I can't barnacle myself to any party or body, I become invisible. But like a microbe, invisible and worrisome.

The Kosmos Hotel was built by the French for the 1980 Olympics. It's a half-hour by taxi from Red Square. There is no place you'd want to set out to on foot. I can compare the area only to a vast and underdeveloped industrial park for scale and cosiness. Like Imperial Rome, the scale of newer Moscow is for humans who are either very much out of the ordinary or inhabiting a notional space much grander than mine.

March 3

Somersault back to March 3 and the arrival at the Moscow airport. Winnipeg's airport is in the final stages of renovation. So far it appears unworkable and unattractive. Toronto's airport, from where we crossed the Atlantic unaccompanied by our luggage, is chaotic and inefficient. At 9:00 p.m. when we landed in Moscow the airport was empty. A grand building, marble and granite, spotlessly clean and modern, was not what we'd been given to expect.

Behind a line of wickets stood soldiers or guards or customs officials. It's hard to know. Here the best-dressed people wear uniforms and the variety is endless. We were passed through the line by officials who looked carefully at each passport and at each face. The next point was the baggage check. Bags were x-rayed. I was required to open my hand luggage, then motioned on. I was in the Soviet Union.

Remember, it's March 6 but I'm writing about March 3 so three days into Russia will have given me sufficient time to make comments which extend beyond entry and customs scrutiny. Now there's a palpable tension sifting over the people I'm with. It's this strange, strange country. This foreign and isolated world has breathed on us and the caraway scent doesn't quite mask a breath that carries something hostile. Westerners come here, are fascinated by the country; some loathe it, are frightened by it. Some find it so impenetrable that they can do no more than bump against it and glance off its surface. But its power and impact are unmistakable whether you want to participate or not. It makes people uneasy in their cloth. It narrows the eyes and sharpens elbows and shoulders.

There's something here I want to reckon with. I've heard the sounds being piped, I've heard the song and Russia's caraway-scented breath is mixing with mine. Now I need to know why. I've travelled a fair bit and I've read, but that can't explain why I feel I've seen some of this place before. The exercise I've set for myself is to unwind what's known through familial traces and what I know some other way. Ahead of me lies the task of endless writing so that it's all out. Then the sorting and labelling, the taxonomy must begin. Aristotle did a naming, and Linnaeus. I wonder—did they ask if the naming called up the being or did the finding come first? Were they technicians or alchemists? Conjuring can find you sharing a crucible with strange elements. And I ask myself, do I have so much ease or so little ease inside my own skin that I'm not at odds with this place? Wandering around this monstrous hotel, alone, at night, or drinking vodka from a tumbler, alone in an over-sized bar, the only solitary person there, carrying my situation with me so thoroughly that the appropriate perception of alone simply can't be conjured up, will not be produced. My sense of being in place, in this place becomes an object, fly-in-amber, the metaphor fitting the location. Is it the brutalized spirit or the resilient spirit? Nothing to lose, nothing more to give away, nothing can be taken. And then do I begin again—limestone in liquid suspension, not fly-in-amber this time—to stalagmite another life? Children go, dogs, dear for many years, die. Everything goes. The Russians know that. Their forbearance may recognize the folly of building. Let the State do that. Let Them do that. Monuments imply a lack of faith.

So we're staying at the Kosmos Hotel, certainly no one's first choice. It's the second largest hotel in the world. In the same way that assembly-line, mass-produced goods bear no resemblance to hand-worked embroidery, this hotel pays no mind to elegance and detail. One of the dining-rooms, the one to which we have been assigned, has the cosiness of an airplane hangar. The service is buffet, the quantities plentiful enough to fill large vats. Flavour and texture slide into each other as you jostle through the queue. But there's enough and it's nicely, if coarsely, seasoned. The rooms are fine—brown, rather dimly lighted like everything except the theatres. This must be a preference because there's plenty of electric power. The bathrooms are clean and there are enough towels although they're rough and unmatched. Bed linens too are clean and the rooms warm. There's an honest lack of pretension which I find likeable.

We arrived at the hotel just after 9:30. The lobby was mobbed. We all had confirmed reservations. Three hours passed while our papers—visas and passports—were carried from one desk to another. There's a dance, a certain ritual which must be performed and there's no circumventing or shortening it. You just wait it through, which we did, tired but in good humour. We found a little bar under the stairs, had espressos and waited. Then to our rooms and bed.

March 4

Buffet breakfast, same dining hall each day, a good breakfast: lots of sliced, sour brown bread and sweet butter stamped out in flower rounds, pickled vegetables which I found too formidable for morning food, cold meat, one kind of pale sliced cheese, a thin yoghurt drink, pans of eggs cooked in their shells, rolls, one kind of jam, blinis, porridge and tea. There's no fresh fruit and, we were later to discover, virtually no fresh vegetables, either. And breakfast would be the same each day.

We purchased air tickets to Odessa. All the others bought round-trip tickets. For some reason I was sold only a one-way ticket and trouble followed later. When you travel within Russia you don't use the grand Sheremetyevo airport. So off we set by taxi for the domestic airport some distance away. We were told not to bother purchasing roubles yet. Foreign currency, U.S. dollars, was fine.

This grey, dark building certainly didn't look like the Sheremetyevo. We checked our bags, entered the cold, dark lobby, and were told the flight would be two hours late. We couldn't return to the hotel, too far and anyway we'd checked out. Russia's unique bureaucratic nature was about to make itself known to us directly.

Well, here we are, an amicable group, travelling together, sharing an adventure—what's next? Good—a restaurant overlooking the tarmac. We'll eat and drink and visit. Push the tables together, round up extra chairs, put your coats here—what will you have? No roubles was what we had and no hard currency accepted. But there's a Beryozka shop, a tourist shop, in the lobby and it accepts foreign currency. We'll go down there, make some small purchases and get our change in roubles. No change in roubles—foreign currency only. And, as I came to learn whenever I made a purchase in hard currency, the change you get is whatever they have. So my purse would be full of Deutsch marks, francs, gilden and yen, as well as roubles and U.S. dollars. I've been given more interesting and bulkier change too. At the coffee bar one morning when I had missed breakfast in the dining hall, there simply wasn't change for a $10.00 American bill. To get change the cheery man behind the counter had an alternative. More capitalist businessman than I would have expected, he suggested I make some purchases. The transaction would result in the necessary change. "Why not buy a tin of caviar to take home?" He showed me his teeth which were nicely capped in silver. All I really wanted was coffee and a poppyseed bun. At the end of the transaction I had coffee, the requested bun, a tin of caviar, some U.S. change and a second poppyseed bun. That evening in the foreign currency bar I had a glass of Georgian wine. My change was some U.S. bills, some francs, a box of matches and a chocolate bar. Very good it was too.

Back to the airport, as if we could have left it so easily. We were hungry. What would we do for two hours? And we knew that the delay meant difficulties at the Odessa end. Theatre begins early and we didn't have guaranteed tickets.

Robert and I suggested a picnic. We would go to the Beryozka shop and buy whatever was there. Vodka, bottles of warm tonic, tinned Danish hams, biscuits, salted almonds and chocolates. The shop gave us some paper to spread on one of the little tables in the waiting room; we borrowed a bottle-opener from them; Royal Winnipeg Ballet's André Lewis had a Swiss army knife for slicing the ham; the tins had their own keys for opening and we were set. Drink a little of your tonic water and top it off with vodka. Vodka on tonic. It was perfect. It passed the time, lifted the spirits and filled the stomach. Finally it was time to go to the departure lounge.

In this airport it appeared all the officials were women. We entered a small anteroom. We had our visas and passports examined. Hand luggage and purses x-rayed, we walked through a security arch and into the waiting room. All of us except for André Lewis. For some reason his visa wasn't acceptable and he wasn't going to be allowed to pass. He's not a large man. Slender and blond with a small boy's look of waiting about him, he sat down in a straight chair against a wall while each successively larger female official examined and rejected his visa. He, of all of us, was essential here. He was to dance with Evelyn Hart at the gala concert. The women we've encountered, from theatre ticket-takers to cleaning staff, officials and shop clerks, all shout. Discussion became noisy. Volume and volubility increased. Marvin Terhoc, who headed the "24 Hours" team, is not a small man. He interceded and despite his size got swept into the noise. What had always worked in Canada when a mix-up or a bureaucratic bumble had occurred didn't seem to apply here. Beyond the difficulty of language was a different mind-set. Increasingly in Canada, there's less willingness to be officially flexible but still there's the chance, the prevailing belief, that if you explain the situation with enough clarity reason will prevail and exceptions will be made. Not here. The operative phrase: "Not possible." Our flight was about to depart. None of us would leave without André but this is not a country where you decide to change plans. We were expected in Odessa, we were expected out of Moscow. What now? Well, someone decided that a change of decor was in order. Not decorum, just decor. Men began carrying in large upholstered desk chairs. Over their heads, through the knot of people at the entrance and into the tiny space, they began to introduce the chairs. Four or five were brought in. Without interrupting the rhythm of their harangue, the women officials began trying them out, a sort of cacophonous, bureaucratic musical chairs. Finally even they were struck by the absurdity of the dance because they stopped in mid-production, the dancing ceased, chairs were pushed to the side, some chairs were carried back out and after an official-sounding call to the Canadian embassy by Marvin, André was deemed acceptable, allowed to pass and we boarded our first Aeroflot flight.

The stewardesses were sturdy, sensible-looking women and they wore overcoats and mufflers. The flight took two hours. There was no in-flight service. This might have been a bus. The bonus—no smoking. As the flight drew to an end, lottery tickets were offered on a tray for purchase by Soviet citizens. Tourists were told to exit first. We walked a short distance across the ice-pocked tarmac to a bus which took us several yards to the terminal. We collected our bags and I was met by an Intourist driver and car for the trip to the hotel. I shared the car with another tour-less individual, the wife of Southam's Russian Bureau Chief. The others travelled to the hotel by bus.

The Chernoe Hotel reminded me again that time has a different measure in the Soviet Union. The American, Lincoln Steffans, travelled to Russia just after 1917. He returned to the United States and he pronounced, "I have seen the future and it works." I'm not a student of political science and I'm not a seer so I'd be unable to draw any conclusions about the future or about the success of Communism. From here, now, things seem to be working. That is, no one starves, no one is on the street except by choice and those people are few, the literacy rate is high and the Moscow subway system, a source of pride. And I don't really know how it was before. I fear a levelling off because it always means a levelling down. At the same time I believe without hesitancy that everyone should have access to a good education, the best medical care, to green spaces and light, to shelter and enough food, to freedom from abuse and to the opportunity to formulate the wish for more.

Odessa and the Chernoe Hotel raise the question of time. They're from another time, a time Russia denies while using it and this seems a dishonesty.

I need to sort and sift here, not inappropriate when speaking of time—sands and all. It appears the State calls the shots, the State somehow separate from the people. And the State has set up vertical time zones. There's the future and in this compartment belong the space program, defence and the children. There's the present. Adults live here. Workers, bureaucrats, old women on the streets sweeping with twig-bundle brooms, visitors and people doing business all occupy it. Then there's a more interesting time, the time that's caught my fancy and has me musing. For one thing, it slides. It starts in the past, not the anthropological bone-and-artefact past of archaeology, and not the early Russia-establishing, hordes-across-the-steppes past. I think it started with the westernization by Peter and Catherine because size, geography, oriental proximity, mystical Rasputin-black moustaches and caviar-dark eyes aside, Russia is leaning, yearning, facing, bending west.

My mother has an antique gold watch-chain. On it is a small gold catch set with opals. This catch or slide rides up and down the chain, settling on your neck wherever you choose. In Russia, in my short visit here, time appears like that watch-chain's opal slide. No lateral movement, just up and down with ease. Up to the future, slip back to the past.

Odessa sits at the western tip of the Black Sea, Russia's Riviera. Its climate is moderate, Mediterranean, except this year, the coldest since before the Revolution. The architecture and the set of the streets give the appearance of a nineteenth-century city. Not many tall buildings, not many new buildings. Like Deauville in Normandy, the seaside location speaks of vacations, leisure, lightness and frivolity but even sparkling, expensive Deauville is unwelcoming in the off-season. So here, I adjusted for summer light. I greened the trees, lightened everyone's heavy clothing and straightened bodies bent against the cold wind. I looked at the nineteenth-century neoclassical and art nouveau-laden architectural structures tinted the colour of summer ices: rose, yellow, lime, blue. I looked at the beautifully proportioned tree-lined streets and tried to lift the veil, the gauze, the net, the muslin of grey, and I couldn't, quite. Two days later now back in Moscow I was to visit the Pushkin Museum and there I saw one of the meanest, least charitable paintings I've seen, called *The Old Coquette*, by sixteenth-century painter Bernardo Strozzi. In the painting a grey-haired old woman, once beautiful, sits before a dressing-table mirror. Her back is toward us. Age has accumulated ridges of flesh at her neck. In the mirror her face, distanced in years and space, is a little younger but the bosom sags, the shoulders slope. Her fingers are too knobbed with arthritis to wear rings. She's attended by two miserable young women who appear to be ridiculing her in the preparation of her toilette. She belongs to a time of frivolity and decadence, of cities which provided pleasure and services for the wealthy. The coquette appears to have outlived her usefulness. She is not, however, dead. She's just guilty of a lapse of good judgement and tastelessly, indiscreetly, she carries on. She is Odessa.

The dishonesty I talked about earlier, Russia's dishonesty about time, is that while Odessa clearly speaks of a time now out of favour—that time space is still being exploited. The contract North Americans have with time is a warranty, a guarantee that soon, or eventually, the thing won't work, will have to be discarded and replaced. Obsolescence we understand. It's annoying because waste is a bad thing but we understand it. Everything has its time. But here, well, what about here? I'm not terribly comfortable in Russia. The hotels are dreary, the food is dreary since most meals are eaten in the hotels. Everything is difficult, the operative phrase here when you ask for anything, anything, is, "It's not possible," but I'd like to stay, feel I need to stay until I can get a handle on this time thing.

It's everywhere around me—the vehicles on the street, for instance. People appear to be driving vintage cars and trucks and it's not because they're hobbyists driving lovingly restored cars in a Kinsmen parade on Sunday. A lot of the cars and trucks are really old and are used here as a matter of course, still breathing, still moving.

And we were at the Bolshoi Theatre. Their ballet company danced. It was a ballet I didn't know. I assumed from costumes, sets, music and story that it was a piece contemporary with Tchaikovsky, certainly pre-1917. Not at all. It's a relatively new ballet. What an astonishing thing, I thought, since the piece wasn't an historical allegory or a satire. Just a copy from a period that's been completely erased. Except in the theatre, I guess, and the next question is—why would that be? But I'm getting out of time. I haven't been to the Bolshoi yet because I'm still in Odessa.

Odessa. Our hotel, the Chernoe, had unspeakably depressing

public rooms but the bedrooms were quite pleasant, homey almost, with stringy plants staked in odd containers at each window and little pieces of worn oriental-style carpet runners. The rooms were like old train compartments with narrow beds built against the walls, a small, shaky writing table and chair, a shallow closet with two shoe brushes, three hangers and a bathroom, the whole of which became the shower stall simply by intending it. That is, there was a tiled floor which sloped to a drain in the centre and a shower and taps on the wall. Very efficient and likeable.

Since our flight had been delayed we were terribly rushed. We were to have had a little supper arranged for us by the Intourist guide assigned to us. We were led to the dining-room. Mid-way through the strange little meal our Intourist person flapped up to me and accused me of not having a return air ticket. Well, I hadn't one, I guess. I had done what I was told to do at the Service Bureau in our hotel in Moscow but that turned out not to have been enough. I must hurry down to the Intourist office in the lobby immediately and purchase a return ticket or be left behind. That ever-present threat—being left behind, behind the others, behind the eight ball, behind the Iron Curtain.

Without any difficulty, which at this point expressed itself as a void, I bought my airline ticket. The timey, sandy print, the void was soon filled as another problem seeped in. The others had rushed off to the Odessa Opera House where Evelyn Hart was performing *Giselle* with Andris Liepa, already a legend at twenty-two. There were absolutely no tickets. Robert and I were late.

Too late for a taxi. Point us to the Opera House. At a trot, in biting wind, over rutted streets, in the dark, going nowhere with any certainty, we hurled ourselves down the strangest street I've travelled. It was beautifully tree-lined. The air smelled of must and paprika and the leafless trees bore strange, strange fruit—blackbird blossoms. Every branch of every tree was heavy with dark brown blackbirds who rustled and muttered in the night light—all over Odessa, up and down every street as far as we could see.

We stormed the theatre, indicated to one of the legion grandmas who woman all the ticket posts in all the theatres in Russia that we were Canadian. Finally, just as the curtain was about to be raised, we were hurried to two separate but first-rate seats.

The Odessa Opera House is apparently a copy of the Paris Opera House. A nineteenth-century confection, four tiers above the orchestra, the icing a liberal application of gilt-covered plaster swags and rococo embellishments forming a horseshoe with the stage at the open end. The upholstery was in bordeaux velvet. Plaster putti scattered and cavorting about, culminated in cast figures grown larger than life, flanking the stage and insinuating themselves around the topmost curtains, which themselves were richly embroidered with gold thread. The ceiling was decorated with painted scenes framed in elaborate gold cartouches and an enormous crystal-prismed chandelier dominated the centre. No one's gown could have competed with the dazzle of that theatre, not even in *La Belle Epoque*, and certainly today any such effort would be futile.

March 13

I'm still trying to write myself out of Odessa. Part of the delay or the long-taking is because the days here are full and like everyone I'm travelling with, I find myself exhausted and craving sleep whenever I return to my room. The writing feels good. I'm glad to be doing it because it's part of the scratch to get at the under-skin feeling I'm having about Russia. But a fatigue fills my lungs like a fully taken breath and I must sleep.

March 4
Odessa Opera House

Evelyn Hart was a fragile, fevered Giselle, frail and too quick to live a life full out. Her partner, the Prince, Andris Liepa, the son of the famous Marius, blond and beautiful, slight and delicate in street clothes, was athletic, powerful and tall on stage. The supporting dancers were an interesting mix. The men were strong, vigorous and more dramatic than Canadian dancers. The female corps members were larger too, but here size didn't serve as well and for the most part they were bulky and almost clumsy. Tonight's *Giselle* was a more theatrical performance of this ballet than I've seen done in Canada by either the Royal Winnipeg or the National Ballet.

The opera house was full and the audience, while they appeared to enjoy themselves, seemed to take their role seriously. They were a mix of ages, well dressed, attentive and likeable as a group of spectators and I enjoyed sitting in their midst.

The second act was even stronger than the first. A superbly melodramatic encounter between Giselle's rustic suitor and the Queen of Death and her attendants—wonderful, hammy and played out in full. Evelyn Hart, ephemeral as a fleshly Giselle, was pure spirit when dead. The eye had to question whether her feet actually touched the stage.

But early in the second act the corps de ballet performed a silly movement. Rows of women facing and moving in alternate directions, bodies bent at the waist, each with a leg extended parallel to the floor, hopped out of sync in a parody of symmetry. The repetition and order gave witness to politics' shaping an audience's taste as they applauded enthusiastically what was essentially a ragged movement.

After the performance Robert and the others had work to do backstage and I sat in the lobby and waited and watched the opera house empty. Then the lights were turned out and I sat in the cold, dark foyer of a grand, gold opera house in a city which is being left to slide and crumble, and watched as the mists from Act II's graveyard scene swirled around my ankles and I was transported out of my present more effectively and quickly than I could have been on any sound-whining jet.

March 5

Still Odessa, but up early for the return to Moscow. Here we've joined up with Robert Barclay's film group and we'll all return together. We had breakfast in a room set aside for our group, and Robert and I shared a table with Evelyn Hart and Galina Yordanova, who is Evelyn's teacher and friend. Galina lives in Bulgaria and speaks Russian so her surroundings don't mystify her the way they do us. She explained that each year she travels to Winnipeg for a time to work as a teacher with the Royal Winnipeg Ballet, maintaining the ties with the Russian method which Arnold Spohr established for his company in the 1960s. Evelyn was exuberant, appropriately pleased with last night's performance, and was irrepressible. Off-stage she's little and gamin, on-stage she commands and controls.

By the time we'd flown from Odessa to Moscow, been met and transferred to the hotel, checked back into the hotel, had a little to eat from the lunch buffet, found a taxi, and arrived in the centre of Moscow, the day was almost over—cold, windy, snowing, darkening and almost over. Everything here takes so much time. There isn't room in this country for the frivolous gesture. Each step must be as deliberate as if it were encased in those insulated and legendary felt and rubber boots I've seen here on the feet of the very young and the very old.

Barclay's group, now increased in number by the addition of the "24 Hours" people, was moved around everywhere by a full-sized red and white Intourist bus complete with guide. Our guide had presented herself in the lobby of the Chernoe Hotel in Odessa. Her name was Zena. She was short and tidy, pretty, with long brown hair. When she met us that first time she wore a full-skirted dress with wide sleeves which closed in narrow cuffs. Her hair was attractively arranged, she seemed young and pleasant and open. While she never lost her temper or even displayed real annoyance, that first occasion was the only time I would describe her as I have. From that time on she wore a wool cloche pulled low over her forehead and a woollen overcoat with a fur collar—very stylish. I can't remember if the ensemble was brown or grey. The sole exception to this Intourist habit was made on the night of Evelyn Hart's gala concert. I don't recall what she wore because I was so startled to find her without her hat, hair loose and considerably flattened from having been kept under wraps, as it were. She was with the group constantly. Every group is assigned an Intourist guide, I believe, but her presence came to seem ubiquitous, especially since, toward the end of the trip, she delivered a bald-faced propagandistic lie. More of that later.

Our group was not a tourist group. The visas, with the exception of mine, were working visas. I'm sure that a group of foreign journalists and film-makers on visas so identified would not have been assigned a novice guide who would have been guilty of lack of guile or the appropriate vigilance, *glasnost* or not. Zena appeared willing to help and accommodate so long as our requests coincided precisely with her predetermined agenda. In other words, cleverly, not at all.

Because my visa was marked tourist and because I was travelling as an individual I was met at every turn by transportation which was provided for me alone. It certainly was convenient but I really didn't have an inclination to be separated from Robert. At the domestic airport in Moscow I was met on my return from Odessa by a black limousine of '40s vintage, a splendid thing but a little sepulchral to enter alone. The Intourist representative who met me couldn't understand why I would prefer travelling in the bus to having my own car and I didn't, so long as Robert could come with me. Yes he could, so off we drove, but our bags would follow with the others on the bus. We arrived at the Kosmos Hotel long before they did. As an individual, I could check in but Robert couldn't do that independent of his group and since my bags were with the group's and I wasn't, I had to be on the spot to ensure that they were delivered to my room. So we waited. Ordinarily I don't wait well. I'm not especially patient but in Russia I found myself doing it with ease. It's just so much a part of the unusual and specific rhythm of this country. Strange music—a hesitation, some forward movement, pause, rush, pause and stop. I'll listen to twentieth-century Russian composers when I get home to see if they've reflected this tempo.

When we were finally able to taxi into Moscow's centre we asked, of course, to be taken to Red Square. The taxis can't drive right into the square so we were let off at Marx Prospekt. In scale it's vast enough for tank parades to circle in front of huge crowds. Russian scale—determined by geography and political intent.

Red Square lies off Marx Prospekt behind a little rise in the land so it reveals itself to you at whatever pace you approach it. We walked slowly since we weren't entirely sure where we were going and then the Christmas-candy, Fabergé-egg, Byzantine-cloisonnéd domes began to rise before our eyes. St. Basil's Cathedral, now a museum, is as improbable a sight as any symbol you've seen reproduced so often you believe it to be only that and not something real. I felt giddy. There it was, and here we were, walking across Red Square, passing in front of Lenin's tomb, approaching St. Basil's Cathedral, in the Soviet Union, and the wrangle and rush to get visas and the distances that had to be flown and bussed and taxied weren't anything to do with being in a place that was so foreign and extraordinary as this. If North America has an enemy we were in enemy country, standing under the same falling snow with people whose lives are circumspect and circumscribed, who plod and forebear, who are supposed to be dangerously at ideological odds with the thinking of the governments of Canada and the United States, with whom we stand toe to toe, jaw to jaw, taut and bristling with the knowledge that we two differing ideologies, we opposing powers hold the possibility of destroying the world with a nuclear war.

How could Robert and I be standing here? How is it that while I'm here every morning I eat a heavenly, soothing, creamy, sweet porridge prepared for me perhaps by one of the people crossing Red Square, and who is it who launders the poor ragged towels that appear fresh for my bath each morning? These same hostile and dangerous people?

The various kinds of transportation which brought me here and the attendant discomfort, the hours spent in travel, are still not sufficient to account for my having travelled long enough or far enough to bring me to Russia. This place, offering the sense of a country which is unique to my experience and to my imaginings, this puzzle of time that Russia presents, like a sable drawn slowly and maddeningly under my nose, across a bare shoulder, slipping down my arm and then gone, and the perfume of the place, not always pleasant—I'm going to seize it, comprehend it and write it down yet.

A crowd had gathered in Red Square. We joined it and faced the entrance to Lenin's tomb with the others and waited. Inside the square-cut, polished, red granite, one-storey building rested Lenin's mummified body, visible through a glass casket. Nervousness made us whisper to each other "peasant under glass," but very quietly and no laughing please. It was an inappropriate comment. Lenin is much revered and his name and face appear everywhere, over and over, on buildings, monuments, billboards, flags, collar buttons, streets and squares and, of course, in the beautiful city once called Petrograd.

Two grey-coated soldiers flanked the entrance. Three others appeared, from where, we hadn't noticed. With measured stride they approached the entrance. The two guards at the door were replaced by two new guards who moved slowly, rhythmically. The departing guards faced their two replacements. They tenderly brushed the snow from their comrades' shoulders, turned up the collars on their coats and then the three soldiers hoisted their rifle butts vertically to the open palm of one hand and in unison, slow-measured, descended the steps, legs high-striding in a goose-step, free arm swinging pendulum-like diagonally across the body. The precision of the choreography and the movement was such that their changes in direction were imperceptible as they marched clock-work pace the 300 yards to the garrison. Their leather boots, three pairs only, resounded on the pavement with heart-chilling timbre. Multiply that sound to the equivalent of a fascist army and the time slide takes you back fifty years in a second.

The square was full of police and soldiers. We set out across the cobbles for the walk which ran in front of the G.U.M. Department Store. A black-shearling-coated policeman waved us off to the side with a painted truncheon. All the police, grey-coated, black-coated, hold them all the time. At one end of the square sat a small car, blue lights on its roof, motor idling. It was present there, in Red Square, in a different place each time we were there.

The biggest department store in Moscow is the G.U.M. but there must be other, better places to shop because many of the people in the streets, in the hotels and theatres, were well dressed and there seemed to be nothing but the poorest, dreariest goods for sale there. The building is arranged after Milan's Galleria. There's a fountain, iron-work balconies, skylights and crowds of people shuffling slowly past little shops with high-priced, poor quality, colourless goods for sale.

It was snowing and dirty slush accumulated at the entrances. Old women with wooden shovels pushed the slush out the doors and onto the sidewalk while shoppers scuffled it back in. The walkways were wet and dirty and there were at least three tiers of shoppers shuffling in different directions under insufficient light, past goods that were both undesirable and unattainable. Bosch had already painted this scene. And imagine not ever getting your heart's desire and then imagine not ever having a heart's desire.

We needed warmth and some cheer. The famous National Hotel stood across Marx Prospekt, a distance equivalent to four football fields laid end to end. No crossing above ground. The under-street tunnels were dark and wet. It was day's end. People were tired. Everyone walked quickly. There was little conversation. Mole-blind, we hurried across the vast space and emerged beside the hotel.

It's a piece of art nouveau architecture built before the Revolution. The American journalist John Reed, who wrote *Ten*

Days That Shook the World, stayed there and so did Lenin and other heads of government. We had wanted to but couldn't. No groups, individuals only, was the reason which reached us.

The thing about time here is that nothing is altered by modernization. Things are left just as they were built so there are no unhappy interruptions to period architecture. The National Hotel appears to stand as it did at the turn of the century, with its lovely Russian version of Jugendstil ironwork and leaded glass windows intact.

Most of the public rooms are on the second floor behind closed doors which line a rather dark and uninviting corridor. It's somewhat clubby because you have to know they're there in order to find them at all. But we'd been told by friends who'd travelled to Moscow before to seek them out as havens of graciousness and plenty, and after the G.U.M. Department Store and our subterranean trek across Marx Prospekt, we were needing some of that. We wanted cognac and coffee, which is strong and black and excellent in Russia. We searched out the hard currency bar and settled in, talking together about what we'd seen that afternoon. A man, unmistakably American, in a camel-hair sports coat, approached us. He said he was delighted to hear English being spoken. He was from Chicago, a businessman involved in some venture or other with the Soviets, loved the country, travelled here often and was a student of Russian history and culture. Within minutes he'd told us enough for us to feel we'd known him for a long time. Actually, his Midwestern openness was endearing and we were warm and comfortable with our cognacs and coffee. He said he had an appointment but would return in an hour with a friend of his, a Russian woman who worked in the theatre. Would we be his guests for dinner in the hotel? We were intrigued by the possibility of spending an evening with a Muscovite who was not an Intourist guide and we accepted.

He returned in an hour as promised, bringing with him an attractive blonde woman, elegant and slender, who appeared to be in her late 30s. He was a regular guest in the hotel and we were able, therefore, to get a table in the Russian currency restaurant and were given excellent service. Our host told us that often maître d's are surly and perverse and will refuse to seat you in a half-empty restaurant even when you've made reservations. There's no incentive for them to fill their dining-rooms or to be accommodating. This stolidness, a sort of digging-in-heels intractability, is an attitude we came in contact with often. It must be one of the few small revenges against the control which is pervasive in everyone's life.

Robert and I improvised the perfect meal for ourselves, to the astonishment of the waiters, our host and his guest. We wanted only caviar and vodka. We were served a generous bowl of the best soft black caviar in the whole world. With it we had sour black bread and sweet butter and spears of ice-cold English cucumbers and tiny glass after glass of 100-proof Stolychnaya.

Finally, urged by our host, we ordered little pots of mushrooms and beef in cream and then like children had to have the wonderful Russian ice-cream for dessert.

Nina, our host's Russian friend, was charming and elusively unspecific about her work. She did, however, tell us she was a Christian and she showed us a tiny icon she carries in her purse. Her English was perfect. No, she hadn't travelled abroad, she'd learned it as a student in high school and university, and no, she didn't want to travel abroad because she would see too many things she couldn't afford. We sensed from her quick response that there were more than material goods she might see and not be able to afford. She said she found the pace of life in Moscow rushed and too full. This was surprising since there seemed to us to be little in the way of leisure-time options.

It was an interesting evening but like every encounter we had with Russia, this one too left us tired and we excused ourselves by 10:00 and took a taxi back to our hotel, located at the edge of Moscow, the steppes no more than a chilly breath away.

March 6

I spent the morning in the hotel writing and reading and looking out the window of my room on the twelfth floor, down endless, wide streets, more like double-lane highways than streets, which stretched in every direction from the hotel. Since Stalin, every street is wider than Portage Avenue or Main Street in Winnipeg. In Winnipeg these streets, rather than being the gracious boulevarded avenues of Paris or Vienna, are inhospitable. Dwarfing and daunting to cross at any time, the broad avenues become icy, rutted wind tunnels in winter. As soon as I was old enough to travel to major cities, I was embarrassed by our two main streets. All that room could be given over to roads because our urban space wasn't valuable or all that space reflected rude beginnings we never quite grew out of, I felt. In Moscow the breadth of the post-revolution main thoroughfares seems designed to diminish human scale. Here, space appears to reflect something other than Winnipeg's lack of sophistication. That space had become political.

Each day from my window I watched small figures in black move deliberately and evenly paced across these too-broad avenues, across open spaces that set public buildings back from the roadways, across empty lots, not yet supporting one of the endless apartment buildings that lined the streets. They walked along these highways and then queued up to wait for public transport. The buses and subway system are efficient and one of the major tours for tourists is a circuit of all the metro stations around Moscow. Illustrated books about them are available at all the Baryozka shops, but efficient or not it disturbed me to see knots of people standing in the open, next to highways, waiting to be collected. This phenomenon could be witnessed through the day although it was more evident in the morning and evening. There was a surprising amount of movement at night as well and since there seemed to be little night-life I couldn't determine where everyone was going. There was just a prevalent sense of movement whose pace never altered. I watched it from above, from my hotel room, or as I hurried past in a taxi. It was never explained and the fact that I was viewing it from a distance contributed to my sense of its being odd and somehow sinister. But there had to be specific destinations and a purpose to the travel. Idleness is not encouraged or tolerated.

The people we observed who were employed in the hotel worked long hours and a number appeared to be doing the same job with frequent breaks, little enthusiasm, a lot of duplication, repetition and inefficiency. It seems no one can vary the smallest routinized step or make even a minor change or accommodation. Authority to make decisions always lay elsewhere. If it's an assembly line then the belt moves forward, jerks to a stop, arrested momentum making everything slide backward, then the belt slowly begins again, moving hesitantly on.

In the afternoon we took a taxi to the city's centre and got out at the Pushkin Museum. It's counted among the great museums of the world and certainly it has impressive holdings, pieces I thrilled to see, having seen them only in reproduction. There are no concessions made to foreign visitors, no signs or guidebooks in English, or English-speaking guides. Knowing our time was limited we set out at full tilt. We decided to limit our viewing to the Italian and Dutch galleries, fourteenth to seventeenth centuries, and to the French galleries, seventeenth to twentieth centuries. That much we were able to pick up from the floor plan.

The building is grand scale but not large enough for the collection on display. As a result the walls were over-full with some pieces hanging too high for proper viewing or opposite windows in such a way that the light glancing off the surface obscured the viewing. Lighting appeared to be primarily window light which in some cases would save the paintings and in some cases would surely damage them. Humidity control was in the form of narrow pans of water placed on the floor under some of the paintings. A few of the pans were dry. I thought of our gallery in Winnipeg with its elaborate and sophisticated systems for protecting works of art and I looked at a magnificent portrait by Mannerist painter Bronzino and I noticed the pan under it had gone dry.

Like the buildings from the distant past now deemed inappropriate, unnecessary or even dangerous—the churches, the homes of the aristocracy, the fine architecture from the turn of the century—these irreplaceable paintings valuable to all mankind, belonging to all of us and to time, may be in jeopardy, left to make their own way, to deal with time as best they can. My fear is that time is ruthless and not very selective. It's too democratic in its destruction.

The French paintings, early twentieth-century Impressionists and Modernists, were thrilling. Two van Goghs caused a catch in my chest for their brilliant colour, their richness and generosity, and for the tragic life of their maker.

We entered a large room filled almost wall to wall with Impressionist paintings and were startled to see two triptychs, unquestionably by Matisse and of which we had been completely unaware. On closer examination we discovered they weren't triptychs at all, just two groups of three paintings sharing the same subject, year and palette. Lack of hanging space had resulted in an installation which while curious and startling was most probably not what Matisse had in mind.

With an appetite augmented by our art-viewing we walked to the National Hotel where once again we had that exquisite soft black caviar, dark bread and butter, a cucumber, green onion and sour cream salad and vodka. Robert had meetings all evening. I read and wrote and slept.

March 7

I was late coming down for breakfast and the large dining hall was closed. There's a little foreign currency bar under the stairs, very cozy, where one can always be assured of at least coffee. This morning was one of the few happy occasions when they had milk too. So I settled in with good appetite to a breakfast of canned orange juice from Greece, Russian coffee and for the first time poppyseed buns. I read and munched and was perfectly, delightedly content, so content with my improvised breakfast that I decided to have another bun. What ensued was the caviar, two-poppyseed-bun transaction.

It was on this day after lunch that I first attempted to arrange travel to Leningrad for Robert and myself for March 11. The midnight train to Leningrad had been recommended by everyone—romantic, comfortable, a special experience. The recommendation that accompanied this travel information was that an overnight train both ways with a day sandwiched between was tiring and to be avoided. We decided the perfect plan would be to take the train there and fly back. Our visas had been cleared for Leningrad before we left Canada. Robert's work would be finished. There was no reason not to go and the idea of being in Russia and not seeing at least some of the collection at the Hermitage was mad. While Robert worked I would go to the Service Bureau and make the necessary arrangements.

"Could I arrange for travel to Leningrad?"

"Yes of course. You may buy a tour by train both ways for the equivalent of $250.00 U.S. each."

"No—I want to travel to Leningrad via the overnight train, spend the day there and return by air."

"Not possible."

"OK. Then I'd like to fly both ways and stay at a hotel in Leningrad for one night." That would give us almost two days there and would be fine.

"Not possible."

"But we've been told by Canadians living in Moscow that it's done."

"Not possible. See the Excursion Desk and they will arrange it for you."

Over to the Excursion Desk to begin again. I explain what I want, we cover the same area, I'm told again that it's not possible but try the Air and Train Ticket Desk.

Now all this travelling between desks and bureaux took more time than the telling because people were on breaks, or the English-speaking person wouldn't be back until 3:30 so please return then.

In all, I spent the better part of the afternoon being courteous, inquisitive and unsuccessful. Three hours at least, spent knowing full well that what I was asking was possible and that a certain stolid inflexibility or resistance to variation stood between us and the Hermitage.

I indicated that if we would be unable to travel to Leningrad we would leave Russia early with our much-desired hard currency. Foreign currency is sought after but still some tiny bureaucratic nick kept the needle on the record, repeating over and over, "It's not possible."

What a "not possible" difference and how interesting it was to be faced with it! In the West, money makes everything possible. In Russia that's not the case. Free enterprise, entrepreneurship just aren't here.

That night arrangements were made for tickets to see the Bolshoi Ballet Company dance at the Bolshoi Theatre. The theatre is enormous, imposing, elegant, the exterior a pale mustard yellow and white painted stone. The interior of the theatre is like Odessa's Opera House but more elegant, a little more restrained. We sat in a box on the first level and from here I looked out over the orchestra level at the main floor where seating was individual chairs.

So, I thought to myself, here I am in the Bolshoi Theatre in Moscow, waiting for the curtain to go up, and dancing tonight in a ballet called *Anna* was Russia's most famous, most favourite Katerina Maximova. As difficult and brutalizing as this past year has been, life's endless surprises and possibilities still make me want to stand up and cheer. Here, in Russia, especially—cheer for the indomitable human spirit and the way it won't be denied.

The ballet was a surprise. Naturally the printed program revealed nothing to me but at intermission I stepped into the reception area where food and drinks were served and there I met Nina of the National Hotel, Midwestern-American dinner, and she in her perfect, elegant English explained what we were seeing.

What I had believed we were seeing was a ballet contemporary with *Nutcracker* or *Swan Lake*, a turn-of-the-century piece, ornate, elaborate and traditional. Not at all. This was a fairly new ballet, just a year or two old, a recent addition to the Bolshoi's repertoire. And *La Belle Epoque* sets and costumes and posturings were recent creations, pulled from the decadent, unworkable, rejected past and placed in the repertoire of the national ballet company. The contradiction which time presents here was once again making its statement.

The charming fat-bellied male character in the ballet, the one who had the single really interesting part, turned out to be the ballet's choreographer. No fool he! And the other male lead, the thoughtful, sympathetic character, who often danced just at the edge of the stage and carried on an intimate balletic dialogue with the audience, is Maximova's husband.

The ballet was an odd mix of times and styles. The costumes and sets were perfect, the tempo and pacing clever and all the dancers, every one, first-rate. Maximova at forty-eight was implausible, a waif of a girl and then a coquette and throughout, astonishing. Three gypsies danced—strident, flamboyant and exotic, using a shimmering arm movement that was irresistibly provocative.

It was an evening which gave witness to the superb execution of dance but I was left with a disquiet about the choice of time in which the ballet was set, and the style. In the United States during the

Depression, what was popular with movie audiences was not *cinéma-vérité*. What people wanted and what they got was Hollywood presenting a lifestyle lavish beyond the dreams of most Americans even in times of prosperity. People went to the movies to escape the brown and black of their lives. Squalor, dinginess and denial were what they dealt with every day. When they went to the movies they wanted to be transported, at least for a time, out of the undeniable reality of their bread-line, just-making-it lives. Maybe that's what ballet is about in the Soviet Union.

March 8

Sunday, International Women's Day, the Soviet equivalent of Mother's Day except, generously, it includes all women, mothers or not. On entering the dining hall we were given a card with the day's date centred in a sprig of flowers. The inside was blank. Someone could write a message.

After breakfast we took a taxi to Red Square. There we witnessed once again the changing of the guard at Lenin's tomb. A miles-long line of people waited to enter and to pass by Lenin's body. Later in the day, when we drove past on our way back to the hotel, the line was still there. Our mission for the day was to buy flowers for Evelyn Hart. Tonight was the gala concert and she wanted armloads of them to distribute to the other dancers. All the flower shops were closed but we were directed to an open-air market. We instructed the taxi driver to wait and we stepped out into the crowd. Women were selling tulips, mimosa and carnations from suitcases. A single tulip cost $2.00 American. Evelyn wanted an armful. We simply couldn't buy them in the necessary volume but because it was Women's Day people were buying a single flower or two or three or a branch of mimosa and carrying them off to give as a special gift. They carried them unwrapped and you could see the mimosa begin to freeze and droop before the thoughtful buyer had even left the market. Flowers and greenery of any sort were just not seen in Moscow. In some of the windows or in hotel elevator lobbies a few stringy plants would be leaning against the streaky glass, wretched in the dry hot air of the hotels. So the purchase and gift of flowers was a special gesture. That night at the gala concert, as people came forward to present a single flower or small bouquets to the dancers, their generosity touched me and reminded me that the selfless impulse, a gesture without return, prevailed as part of the human character.

The gala concert, the impetus for our trip to Russia, was held in Tchaikovsky Concert Hall on Mayakovsky Square. It's the location for the prestigious Tchaikovsky music competitions whose imprimatur is sought by accomplished young musicians all over the world. The hall was built more recently than the Bolshoi Theatre, sometime after the 1920s, I would guess. The inside was circular, painted ivory, with very little gilt embellishment, a classical interior, parquet floors and a round thrust stage. The seats were upholstered in blue and it was tranquil and warm. Sitting in this theatre was like finding oneself shrunk Alice-like to a size allowing for containment inside a Wedgewood Jaspar-ware bowl.

The evening was presented in the form of a recital with a piano accompanist at the side of the stage. Evelyn danced with Andris Liepa again—this time a *pas de deux* from *Swan Lake*. They're a superb pair, displaying a unity that's surprising given the little time they've worked together. In one movement she leaned back, suspended for a second without support. For this attenuated moment she inclined toward him indicating complete trust, a perfect partnering.

Later in the evening they danced a *pas de deux* from the Odessa *Giselle* and again he performed a movement he had done there, something I hadn't seen another dancer do. He leapt into the air and then tossed his arched back backward against itself while airborne, a movement only a virtuoso dancer in absolute control could attempt and carry through. The audience clearly loved them, both as a pair and as solo performers.

Several other couples danced as well; one pair from the Moscow Dance Theatre performed a piece called *Configurations*, choreographed to a piece of music by Bartók. Their strength and skill were apparent even before they began to dance. It was an essential, primordial, brutal piece of choreography, sensual, cruel and absolutely riveting. Given the ballet we'd been seeing in Russia, I thought the audience would have found it too risky and radical. To their credit they recognized it for the extraordinary piece of dance that it was.

The final piece performed this evening was *Le Jazz Hot*. Evelyn danced with the R.W.B.'s John Kaminski. They were outrageous, startling the audience with this unorthodox *pas de deux.* They flirted and teased the audience to wild applause. No one would have objected if they'd danced it all over again.

I'd mentioned earlier that the evening belonged to Evelyn. She earned that ownership by showing the breadth of her virtuosity as much as by her clearly evident skill and intelligence. If we'd seen the best the night before at the Bolshoi then she can step with confidence to her place in their midst.

There was a small party at the hotel but I felt I was getting the flu and I declined and instead went to my room. Robert said he had a few small things to deal with and would come by for a visit later. He was gone a long time and then a knock at the door and there he stood, carrying a tray on which he had wrangled and arranged a bottle of the excellent white Georgian wine, two stemmed glasses, a plate of black bread and butter, a jar of Greek olives, a jar of caviar and some little chocolates for dessert. As we've come to recognize, improvisation is not the mode here and in order to assemble this lovely little midnight supper Robert had to capture the imagination and complicity of the bartender in the hard currency bar. We didn't have a nicer meal the whole of our time away.

Lest you think the day passed without efforts being made to arrange travel to Leningrad—don't be deceived. While not a virtuoso performer, I too have my dance in Russia. It's a ragged piece of choreography that has me pliéing from Service Bureau to Ticket Desk to Excursion Office, a piece choreographed to be danced by Sisyphus, doomed to perform it without cessation. Interestingly, while at the gala we talked to Michael McIvor, C.B.C.'s correspondent in Moscow, who told us our proposed trip was not only possible but his visiting mother-in-law and father-in-law had taken it just a short while earlier.

March 9

The morning after the gala began slowly. We had a leisurely breakfast and once again I made an effort to arrange travel to Leningrad. Our frustration mounts. If we're unable to travel to Leningrad then we must arrange our flight out of Russia soon. It seems the Russians will have their way but we, in our pursuit of art, are just as dogged and we're not ready to give in yet.

Plans were made for the Intourist bus and Zena the Ever Present to carry the two film crews to the centre of Moscow to do some additional site shots and stand-ups. For Robert Barclay the film was possible by having it made as a co-production with *Gosteluradio*, the Soviet national network. Their head of foreign co-production was a charming, urbane man who accompanied the Barclay crew members wherever they went. A film-maker himself, he facilitated the filming on location and acted as the essential buffer and liaison. His wry humour and persistent scepticism made him approachable and credible.

Our first stop for filming was the Kremlin. The day was sunny but with a mean wind. As the bus pulled up to one of the gates in the ten-foot-thick walls, our Russian film-maker indicated to us that we would enter as a group and be counted, and that we must reassemble and be counted again in order to exit. The two film groups agreed to meet at a particular time and then we split up. Robert was to do a stand-up in the area called Cathedrals' Square and as we crossed the Alexandrovsky Garden and walked past the Arsenal and the Council of Ministers Building the golden domes of the cathedrals became visible. Built in the fifteenth century but essentially Romanesque in style, the three cathedrals are startlingly beautiful. I approached the mosaic-covered entrance facades. What I'd thought were Byzantine-style mosaics in a soft palette revealed themselves as fresco paintings. I hadn't seen painting of this sort on exposed exterior surfaces before and had misread them.

Zena offered to escort us the next day so that we could examine the Kremlin more closely and view the interiors of the cathedrals. The misinformation my eyes had given me initially was probably no less accurate than the reading of facts we would get from Zena. Not only did time slide, but perception as well. Where you stood determined what you saw and no one could stand exactly in your footsteps. My sense of unease about the reliability of someone else's reading of Russia was confirmed by a brief incident which occurred on the bus to the Kremlin that afternoon.

To explain I have to go back two nights to the hard currency bar in our hotel. After the performance at the Bolshoi the Winnipeggers had gone there for a drink before bed. While we lounged and talked a young man sitting near us swivelled around to face us and struck up a conversation because he'd heard English spoken. He was from Quebec and delighted to find fellow Canadians. He was a law student who had interrupted his studies in Canada to attend a special language institute in Moscow. He'd been here for several months and his Russian was coming along, but slowly. He played hockey, liked Russia, spoke English with a New Zealand accent since that was where he had learned it and was a thoroughly engaging young man. We talked a little about conditions for students at the universities and the subject of Russian Jews came up. He said everything was extremely difficult for them in Russia since their passports were required to indicate that they were Jewish. He wasn't. The conversation ranged over a variety of topics and a short time later we left.

What he told us didn't surprise me. Each year as Jews all over the world gather around their Passover tables a prayer is said for the safe passage out of bondage for Jews not free to practise their religion in Russia.

Two days later in the bus, Zena took the microphone and, as we passed a church on Moscow's outskirts and very near to our hotel, she began to deliver a talk on religion in the Soviet Union. She said she had been asked about it some days earlier and now she would respond.

There were a number of churches in the Soviet Union. You were free to practise but could then not be a member of the Communist Party. There was a wide range of different religions. None except those with physically dangerous rituals was banned. There were even seminaries in some cases, where studies could be taken. "No one's passport indicates what religion they follow," she added, as though she'd been in the bar with us two nights earlier. So much for accurate delivery of facts.

The question "Can we go inside St. Basil's Cathedral?" received no response and it was Zena who told us that it was not possible to arrange travel to Leningrad except by train. Error in travel can be overlooked. Certainly it's difficult to do here but what about the other misinformation?

The Kremlin was magnificent and I did want to see the interiors, each housing a noted iconostasis. We would return the next day and see them as part of a larger tour which must include stops at six or seven of the most beautiful Metro stations. Each age has its own monuments.

March 10

The chill we all felt inside the walls of the Kremlin lodged itself beyond our souls and was made manifest in a physical way. Most of us had developed flu and cold symptoms and we decided that another day on the tour bus held captive by the microphone-amplified voice of Zena the Untruthful was probably not medically sound. Everyone rested in the hotel, all of us finding this Russian adventure tiring and stressful in ways we couldn't understand.

The one task Robert and I assigned ourselves was a final assault on the Travel Bureau. Even caught up as we were in the Russian habit of endless and unvarying repetition, still, our North American spirits failed to succumb entirely. There just had to be a way. We telephoned Mark Entwistle, Vice Consul at the Canadian Embassy, and explained to him what had transpired over the last three days. I should add here that saying we telephoned was not to give proper weight to even that transaction. We never found ourselves able to use the telephone and make the successful contact on the first try, not even room to room within the hotel.

So after some time Robert got through to Mark. He said he'd make some calls for us to determine if indeed travel to Leningrad was out of the question for us. A short while later we had our answer. "Not at all." He had spoken to the woman who was head of the Intourist Bureau for Canadians and she said flying both ways was entirely possible. We were to mention her name and to call her directly if we encountered further resistance.

Duly armed, we stormed the Excursion Desk and told our story to the same stolid individual as if it were for the first time. With barely contained pleasure we waited for the standard response. Lips pushed forward in a reproving moue, she pronounced, "It's not possible."

Aha! We sprang. We said the Head of Intourist Canada had said yes we could. To her credit her face didn't even pinken. She just reached for the appropriate forms and began filling them out. Flight to Leningrad and return, for two, and we wanted a hotel for one night. Here her disappointment-dulled eyes flickered. "No," she said, "I can't book a hotel for you now. You should have started three days ago." She figured she had us.

In unison we rose from our chairs. With one voice, a loud one, we said, "We were here three days ago and two days ago and yesterday and you know it!" Beaten, she fell back, feathered pinions fluttering faintly at her breast. With her final strength she lifted the telephone receiver. We'd won! We'd succeeded in tying a knot in an inch of the bureaucratic tape, naturally red here. Neither Vermeer nor Vlamink at the Hermitage could stir in our art-loving hearts the joy and warmth we now felt.

We told everyone we met that afternoon that we'd triumphed. We had managed to arrange an expensive and exhausting, too brief and probably frustrating visit to Leningrad for our flu-wracked bodies. What a victory! The others who were already thinking of *la dolce vita* in Amsterdam believed we were mad but wished us well anyway.

March 11

We leave for Leningrad this afternoon. There's still time after packing the small bags we'll take with us for our overnight stay to take a taxi once again to the Pushkin Museum. There were some pieces we wanted to look at again. Then a lovely lunch in the National Hotel Cafe and back to the hotel to pick up our bags and find the car waiting to take us to the airport. We arrived with enough time over to make our way to a small restaurant in a corner of the airport, separated from the rest of the floor by a screen of thriving green plants and decorated astonishingly in the rustic style of a Bavarian beer garden. We had coffee and delicious pastries and waited with pleasure to see Leningrad and the Hermitage collection.

In Leningrad at the airport, another car awaited us. By this time we were becoming such pros in the tourist-Intourist set-up that we walked directly to the most likely looking individual, said "Enright/Walsh transfer" and we were off.

Leningrad delights the eye. Here the scale is less aggressive and there's more light. The Neva River runs through the city. On both sides, set back from its banks by roadways, sit two- and three-storey buildings in pastel colours, a sort of Florence on ice. Large tugs and barges sit in front of these wedding-cake buildings, and ice floes and open water alternately block and reflect their images on its surface.

Our hotel, the Pribaltiskaya, was set out of the centre of the city and once again would not have been my first choice. Built in the late 1970s, it was grand and elegant, all polished granite and marble, soft music, green plants and stylish furniture. It would have been posh in New York or Paris. The rooms were small and dark brown once again, but comfortable. The dining-room, although recommended, was mediocre, menu choices as limited here as in Moscow. We spotted the table next to us enjoying platefuls of fresh vegetables. "We'll have that," we said.

The response: "Not possible. Only for delegation."

March 12

To the Hermitage. We had a full day to spend. Not, however, because our helpful friend in Moscow at the Excursion Desk had arranged it that way. No. In spite of my saying we'd like the last flight out of Leningrad, she had booked us on the 5:00 flight, which meant we had to leave for the airport at 3:00. She'd shown us, and she'd show us more too.

We discovered, when presenting ourselves to the Flight Ticket Desk at the Service Bureau in our hotel in Leningrad, that while we had paid for two return tickets only one seat had been booked. Just an error, of course. But the people in the Service Bureau at the Pribaltiskaya were more obliging and we managed to change our reservations, having noticed just in time the small details of the too-early departure and the one seat short.

So now to the Hermitage. It's daunting in size and practically impenetrable for Westerners. Again, like the Pushkin, no concessions are made for foreigners—no signs in English, no English-speaking guides. And here, like the Pushkin, every doorway is attended by an old woman. I'm convinced they're chosen first on the basis of general crankiness and then on their specific mistrust of people who come to look at art. In the Pushkin one of them had seized my purse and refused to allow me to enter with it because it was too large. I had to check it and, not wanting to be separated from my identification, my passport, visa and American money, I toured the museum for four hours clutching these random bundles, unable to take notes as I usually do because my hands were full of the details and verification of my existence in the Soviet Union.

The Hermitage would require weeks of constant looking, weeks of being on the prowl, up and down corridors and into every gallery. We had only one day so again we had to priorize. We'll start with the Impressionists, move back to the Dutch Masters, then the Italians.

After several false starts up and down storage corridors and back stairs we came upon the nineteenth- and twentieth-century French section, entering back to front from the twentieth century. Two rooms full of Matisse. He took brushes and painted sound and rhythm. He seized movement and, without arresting it, contained it on the canvas. He made colour sing and dance and presented challenges to seeing that hadn't been offered before. Our pleasure in seeing this large body of his work, our intense interest, the way we flew around the two rooms exclaiming to each other must have been contagious or unusual because the sizeable, seated female attendant nodded and smiled at us while we darted from one Matisse room to the next. She must have been reassured that we two mild lunatics would do no damage. Then other painters, all important and exciting.

A surfeit of art and a need for protein nourishment sent us retracing our steps to a sign with a coffee cup on it. We could stand up and snack or we could go into the dining-room and sit down. Foot-weary, we decided on the dining-room. Tables for eight filled a dingy room in need of paint. Each table was set with coffee cups, paper napkins and plates piled with buttered bread on which rested a slice of luncheon meat of an unhealthy pink colour or a small fish or slice of pale cheese. Dessert was also on the table. Stale and dusty-looking sugar-covered sweet buns formed a lopsided pyramid. We were seated at an empty table. We looked at the food and at each other and decided discussion would lead us nowhere. We had to eat if we were to carry on. Four more people joined us, four dark and Eastern-looking men who displayed no more enthusiasm for the lunch than we had shown. We started in. It took a lot of will and a lot of chewing. The coffee helped. As we chewed we looked around. The well-dressed ballet audience wasn't represented in this room, nor the chic Intourist guides. Breugel had painted these rough faces, as unlikely a group of art-viewers as you would expect to find, certainly not the luncheon crowd at New York's Metropolitan Museum. But they were here to see the paintings and the other

Hermitage treasures just like we were and their travel here was probably just as difficult as ours had been.

No need to linger over this meal. Our waitress, whose girth suggested she had eaten whatever remained at the end of each day, was making a circuit of the abandoned tables. She was lifting between thumb and forefinger all the remaining slices of bread and pastries and rearranging them on plates, which she then set down on cleared tables for the next group of eight. By pointing and showing fingers we indicated to her what we had eaten and were charged accordingly.

Our time was running out. The Hermitage collection of Rembrandts must exceed that of the Rijksmuseum in Amsterdam. Let's look for the Dutch Masters. So we did and exclaimed and were alternately made quiet by what we saw. Then two Leonardo da Vincis to which we were drawn because they are extraordinary and even without ready identification, from a distance their special quality called the eye. And since we were now with the Italians I was convinced there had to be some of the work of Caravaggio so that Robert could see for himself. This is a painter who has come to have special significance for us and I wanted Robert to have at least one for his eyes.

In an enormous room filled, crowded, with paintings and people hung *The Lute Player*. Under it was a settee on which sat two old women. Unmindful of the significance this moment had for us, they continued to visit with each other. We didn't disturb them with our viewing, not standing directly in front of the painting, not stepping back or walking away and whirling around to creep up on it to make sure we'd really seen it. And when we'd walked through other galleries and come back for a last look they were still there talking. The piece was evidently one of their favourites too.

We had to leave or we would miss our return flight. There was no point in being sorry. A week would have been barely enough time. We had seen only a small portion of the collection and couldn't believe the richness of even that small bit. This isn't New

York. We won't be back next year but we will be back.

A taxi was difficult to find. We hurried to the hotel, claimed our checked bags and found the driver who was waiting to take us to the airport.

Travel to Russia had stretched the measure of the world for me but two shows which opened in Leningrad while we were there shrank it again. An exhibition entitled *An American Vision: Three Generations of Wyeth Art* was installed at the museum of the Soviet Academy of Arts, and as we searched the back halls of the Hermitage for the route to the Impressionists we came upon evidence of a contemporary French artist. Stacked wooden packing crates stamped with couturier Yves St. Laurent's insignia lined the walls. His work was being shown in a different section of the Hermitage and he was playing to standing-room-only crowds.

That evening we returned to Moscow. We packed our bags and treated ourselves to another private caviar and black bread supper. How else to say goodbye to Russia?

March 13

We had to be up very early this morning. At 5:30 I came down to the lobby looking for a little breakfast, maybe one last bowl of the creamy sweet porridge. The lobby was deserted, not a soul. I was alone for the first time in the over-sized, arena-scale lobby. I'd finally conquered the queues and the crowds. Maybe I'd grasp the scale of this country yet.

The car to the airport was waiting. We'd been told that customs inspection on exiting Russia could be gruelling. We'd prepared our customs sheets meticulously and couldn't imagine difficulties of any sort.

I approached the inspection wicket and handed in my passport and visa. A pale and unresponsive young face looked at me through the glass. He looked at my passport photo, looked at my face, back to my photo, up to my face. "This isn't your picture," he said finally.

"Yes it is," I answered. Was his English good enough to understand that my hairstyle had changed, that my life had changed?

He settled for asking me my name. Satisfied with the answer, he punched his stamp two times and handed me back my passport. My Russian visa wasn't inside and there were no stamps indicating I'd been in the Soviet Union. Had I?

We boarded the KLM flight almost reluctantly, and flew west. I wasn't ready to leave. The stay in Russia, the endless travelling and waiting, the cold, the very foreign environment had been difficult but still I wasn't ready to leave.

Russia isn't a place to visit that's just different from home. It's more like a question than a destination and until the question is answered there's a disquiet, a dissatisfaction. At the same time, Russia was like an island for me—so remote, so removed and isolated, so self-contained that it presented itself almost as a haven, a unique opportunity to get at my own measure. I'm not sure what it is I took from that country. I was easy there and I don't entirely know why. I'll certainly seize any excuse to return.

We arrived in Amsterdam without incident and as we rode in the bus to the American Hotel I was struck by the quality of the light, the size and clarity of the windows, the random pace of the people moving in the streets and by the colour everywhere—clothing, shop windows, signs, flowers.

Robert bought me a dozen white tulips. We ordered avocado salads and ate even the garnishes on the plates. We had tomatoes at breakfast and cream with our coffee. We went to the Rijksmuseum and saw more Rembrandts and to the Stedlijk and saw more art. We bought art books and catalogues and ate Indonesian food. There was no snow on the streets. People laughed and jostled each other on the sidewalks and teenagers were silly and had purple and orange hair. And I missed Russia. I still do.

A Sense of Wonder

About June 14 of every year it's time to see about wild strawberries. I always drive north because the seasons when I'm not living in Winnipeg I'm living in Gimli and it's north. I know between Gimli and here and I know a little north of there. I mean really know, like the fine, tickling distinction between *savoir* and *connaître* that you learn in high school. *Je connais* Gimli. It was Mommy and Gramma and me, and then it was Mommy and me, and later it was Mommy and my daughter and me but the strawberries and their situation didn't change.

We would head north to check out the berry prospectus. How many, how far along were they and where were they most abundant this year? Where was the patch of substance? As we rounded the curve on Highway 8 that indicated we were four miles south of Gimli, my mother would begin to drive with two wheels on the gravel shoulder. Leaning out the window, I'd scan the ditches as she slowed. The earliest berries ripened where they were most exposed, out on the flat bed in the clay, open to the sun and the dust. "Stop!" It was always a frantic cry as though we hadn't been expecting to stop at all. We jumped from the car. The door on my side was hard to close because the car was pulled so far out of the traffic lane that it rested at a 45-degree angle. I had to push against gravity which I'm convinced is a more active force on the prairies. It accounts for the flatness. We picked wild strawberries into mayonnaise or peanut butter jars. Anything wide-mouthed and shallow. The jars had to be small. Too many berries crushed the ones from the middle down and made them wet. But the first trip out wasn't for serious picking. It was to get the early few and to reconnoitre.

The serious picking began nearer to the end of June if things went as expected. Then you returned to the areas that had offered promises. You kneeled and picked. You spread long grass to find the fullest, reddest berries at the bottom, growing on long stems, taking their time. You checked the ground for ants, you pulled down your shirt and you lay out on your stomach, eye level to the berries, and you smelled them and the damp clay and the growing green.

If the weather had been just right, if there had been rain around the middle of June so the berries could fill up and you found them, you could each fill six or eight jars in the morning before it got too hot. You drove home, pulled off your damp, long-sleeved shirt, your jeans with the mud-stiffened knees, the hot wool socks and old sneakers. You washed in soap flakes in the bathroom sink to guard against poison ivy and then you sat down and spread out your pick on yesterday's newspaper to hull these pin-points of sweet red pleasure.

Here's where the sense of wonder comes in. Because the whole point of this little story is to illustrate a sense of wonder which takes me through the journals to today.

We always set aside enough berries for a fruit nappy full, each. The rest would be made into jam. Practically the first solid food both my babies ate was wild strawberries. A fat-cheeked kid sitting in a high chair with a bowl of berries on the tray in front. Each, as though the knowledge had been passed between them, would pick up a berry between thumb and forefinger and one at a time, silently, blissfully, swallow them down.

Through the winter that followed each strawberry season we'd husband our jam, serving it like a benediction to close family and friends we really loved. If someone were ill we'd take them a jar. We knew what worked.

We didn't plant the strawberry vines, or tend them, but we picked them, pick them every year, and they always taste the same. They're there, they're gifts and they're always the same. That's the sense of wonder.

It's a feeling I have a lot. The point is—my wonder about wild strawberries, blue jay feathers, glittering snow crystals that get caught in my dog's muzzle and sit there like jewellery, some violin concerti, new potatoes fried in butter, air travel, all travel, Robert's moustache, my kids and on, thank heavens, and on—is like my sense of wonder at where I am now.

The prairies are my home. A lot of prairie people have been interested in mark-making, leaving tracks on our map-flat terrain. The journals gave me an opportunity to look over my shoulder. Behind me, on the page, were my tracks. I could set a course for the future from the imprint I'd left and looking back would tell me where I'd been. What I would have to decide was the direction I'd take from here.

When I sat in an opera box in the Bolshoi Theatre in Moscow in March of 1987 life's endless possibilities made me want to call out in full voice, to open my throat and let the joy be expressed in some odd, round, bell-like sound. I was struck by the improbability of my life and have taken note that in all likelihood that's not an accident. It may be that that's my preference. In any event the tracks can only tell me where I've been. For the rest, if I'm lucky, I'll count on the little points of light, the intermittent prairie houses dotted in the snow like my persistent, quirky sense of wonder. I'll follow the dots. I'll draw a line and go from there.

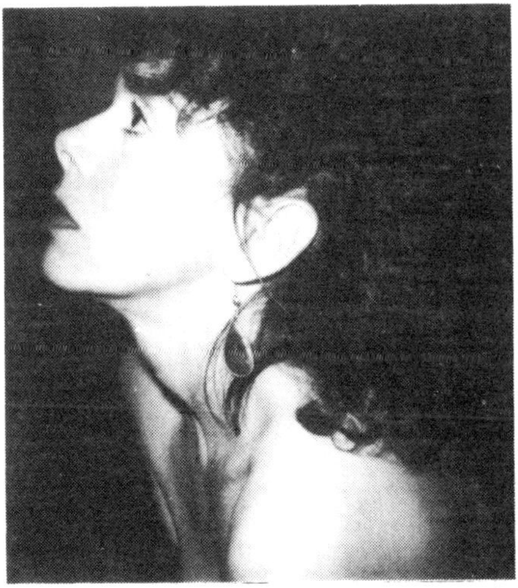

Photo: Robert Enright

Journalist and art critic Meeka Walsh won the Gold Medal in Art History when she graduated from the University of Winnipeg in 1984. In 1988 her article on visual artist Don Reichert won a Gold Medal in the Western Magazine Awards. Meeka Walsh lives and works in Winnipeg, where she is Assistant Editor at *Border Crossings*, a magazine devoted to the arts. She is currently working on a collection of short stories.